YOUR
clever baby

YOUR clever baby

Dr Carol Cooper

with photography by Daniel Pangbourne

RYLAND
PETERS
& SMALL

LONDON NEW YORK

To three awesome young men

SENIOR DESIGNER Sonya Nathoo
SENIOR EDITOR Henrietta Heald
LOCATION RESEARCH Emily Westlake
PRODUCTION MANAGER Patricia Harrington
ART DIRECTOR Anne-Marie Bulat
PUBLISHING DIRECTOR Alison Starling

STYLIST Catherine Woram

First published in the United Kingdom
in 2007 by Ryland Peters & Small
20–21 Jockey's Fields
London WC1R 4BW
www.rylandpeters.com

10 9 8 7 6 5 4 3 2 1

ISBN: 978-1-84597-368-1

A CIP record for this book is available from
the British Library.

Printed and bound in China.

Neither the author nor the publisher can
be held responsible for any claim arising out
of the use or misuse of suggestions made in
this book. While every effort has been made
to ensure that the information contained in the
book is accurate and up to date, it is advisory
only and should not be used as an alternative
to seeking specialist medical or other advice.

contents

HOW CLEVER IS YOUR BABY?

Look around you and you will see that all babies are different. Some are contented, rarely crying, while others seem to alternate between grizzling and screaming. There is also a wide variation in physical appearance, with long lean babies at one extreme and chubbier, chunkier versions at the other. These are the characteristics that parents talk about most often. Babies' looks and their need for comforting are important, of course, because they affect those first interactions between parent and child – and they also have an impact on the amount of sleep you will be allowed to get.

The next thing parents are likely to discuss is how clever their baby is. Cleverness is after all what will help a child to shine at school in years to come, and to do well in life. In this fast-paced and competitive world, intelligence helps an individual to succeed. How clever your baby is determines whether he or she will excel in a career and, if you are very lucky, support you in your old age.

What exactly does cleverness mean? Being clever is not just about reading at an early age, doing advanced sums or passing IQ tests with flying colours. It is also about having emotional intelligence, that combination of common sense and social skills without which special talents can wither on the vine. This kind of all-round cleverness is what helps a baby grow into a well-balanced child and then

into a positive young adult ready to take advantage of a world of opportunities. Clever babies are alert and interested in things. They want to find out more about their environment and the people (and the animals) in it. They have lively minds and they show interest in communicating. At first this is mainly through body language, but before long they make a variety of sounds that soon become recognizable words. Clever babies frequently make mistakes, to be sure, but they learn from them. Nothing is totally wasted, and every opportunity is put to good use.

The first 3 years of life are not a time of great academic achievement, nor should they be. They are nonetheless enormously important years. Not only do babies pass many milestones and gain in independence during this period, but also their brains grow in complexity with a rich network of brain cells that represent what they have learned so far and determine what they will learn in the years to come. By the age of 3, babies have laid down the basis for all their future learning.

Where does cleverness come from? 'He has his father's eyes,' people may remark about a particular child, or maybe the likeness relates to his mother's hair or his grandmother's hands. Like physical characteristics, intellectual and emotional features can be inherited, and sometimes it even seems

obvious which family member they come from. But intellectual and emotional traits are far more complex and therefore less firmly fixed than the simply physical. Newborn babies are never blank slates because they come with their own complete set of genetic material, half from each parent. While there are undeniably advantages of having great genes to start with, nurture plays a key role in intellectual development. If nurture did not matter, then nothing parents did (or did not do) would make a difference. Yet evidence shows that this is not so. Even children with above-average scores in intelligence tests can do even better with the right style of parenting and schooling.

The nature versus nurture debate has raged for years, but the fact is that development depends on both. As developmental psychologists put it, it is a gene–environment interaction. Genes provide the raw material, but you provide the environment that helps to build the structure. There is so much that parents can do to help to fulfil their children's potential, and that is what this book is all about.

Building a healthy body There are many ways to help your baby to become more clever. Good nutrition is a wonderful start. It is important for your baby to be well nourished even before birth, and for long afterwards. Healthy brain development depends on a good supply of essential fats,

protein and minerals. Like the rest of the body, the brain runs on glucose, so getting enough calories is vital too. That is why anyone's concentration can flag when they have not eaten for a while.

Using all the senses Babies thrive on stimulation of all kinds – from touch, vision, sound, smell and taste to more complex forms of stimulation. You provide many of these, but babies find others for themselves. They therefore need to explore their environment without too many restrictions. The baby who lies in a cot or pram most of the day will see and hear very little, and will learn next to nothing. The amount of stimulation must be right for your baby. Too much is confusing and unhelpful. A baby who is bombarded by new things grows bored and restless rather than super-smart. There is no point 'hot-housing' babies anyway, because they cannot learn things before they are ready for them. That is why this book is arranged chronologically from birth to the age of three.

Language When babies learn to speak, they learn what words sound like and what they mean, of course. But they learn to interact socially too. Crucially, language also expands their thinking. Growing word power widens young children's horizons and literally changes their lives. Small words such as 'why' and 'how' become keys with which a child unlocks doors to big ideas.

Movement Physical activity is integral to learning. Although it is possible for babies to learn while scarcely moving a muscle, as some children with special needs are obliged to do, it is easier for babies to learn when they can use their bodies to the full. Developing movement enables babies to learn balance and coordination, and to acquire the hand–eye skills that are needed to manipulate their environment and to make things. Making and building things encourage creativity and facilitate the learning of mathematics and basic physics. Being physically active brings health benefits too, and that in turn promotes an active mind.

You and your love for your baby Babies learn by example right from the start, so what you do as a parent has a profound effect on your baby's development. Even at a day old, babies can imitate adults' mouth movements. Later, they imitate speech. Although babies learn most from hands-on activities, they learn from watching too. In humans, as in monkeys, there are some brain cells that are stimulated when an individual watches someone do something. This may be preparation for the learners to perform the action for themselves one day. In essence, everything babies see their parents do teaches them something, so it is worth trying to be a good role model.

If I had to choose one single thing that would boost a baby's intellect, it would be love. The relationship parents have with their baby moulds every relationship that child will ever have. Love and acceptance from you give your baby the security needed to develop. Strange as it may sound, a cuddle can actually calm a baby's breathing and regulate its heart rate. Love and closeness also boost brain development, especially parts such as the orbito-frontal cortex, which is concerned with social skills. Loving a baby means giving positive feedback and praising when you can. In this way, your baby will have a secure environment in which to learn. It is all right for babies to make mistakes sometimes. You will need to let your baby know when this happens, but also use your love and acceptance as reassurance that it is fine to learn from these mistakes.

CAROL COOPER

milestones

Development is a smooth process rather than a series of hurdles, but parents like to know roughly what to expect when. Not all normal babies reach these milestones at the same age, so they are just guidelines, as are those listed in the charts at the start of each chapter.

Age	Milestone
6 weeks	first social smile
8 weeks	head control improves • practises vowel sounds
12 weeks	plays with fingers • grasps objects placed in hand can reach towards moving objects
4 months	has good head control • babbles and coos • laughs and chuckles
5 months	takes weight on elbows when lying on front rolls from back to side, and side to back can hold an object in hand for several minutes
6 months	reaches out more accurately • sits unsupported shows attachment to parent • may be shy with strangers
7 months	heaves himself forwards on front using arms transfers objects from one hand to the other looks briefly for dropped object • puts together sounds to make two syllables
8 months	grips with finger and thumb • plays on his own sometimes real word-learning starts
9 months	may crawl • points to things • responds to own name understands permanence of people and things

how clever is your baby?

10 months	pulls himself up to standing position • drops things on purpose makes first real word
11 months	stands with support • walks sideways holding furniture • copies parent
12 months	walks with both hands held • can sit from standing position can kiss when asked • uses three words with meaning
15 months	walks unaided • can feed himself with spoon • throws a ball makes tower out of two bricks • begins pretend play • babbles at length
18 months	scribbles • is imaginative • turns pages of a book has on average 40-word vocabulary • makes two-word sentences
21 months	builds a tower of five or six bricks • uses some logic makes three-word sentences
2 years	runs and climbs • puts on socks and shoes • copies a straight line recognizes feeling of full bowels and bladder • is very sociable but has tantrums remembers events of last week and last month • knows own gender uses pronouns and makes plural words • has a vocabulary of about 200 words
2½ years	jumps with both feet • can walk on tiptoe • holds pencil like an adult matches related objects • has sense of body image • is interested in own genitals understands concepts like in, out, up and down • asks 'why?'
3 years	rides tricycle using pedals • climbs well • draws spontaneously • copies a circle knows many colours • may count up to five, and recognizes some letters knows his age • understands almost everything parent says • has a sense of time learns to share and take turns • starts making friends outside the family

how babies
develop and learn

bringing out the best in your baby

The encouraging news is that raising a bright baby requires neither lots of special equipment nor a doctorate in child psychology. Adopting the right attitude and making sensitive use of practical know-how matter much more than expensive new toys or academic qualifications.

Patience and feedback

The key to bringing out the best in your baby is to pay close attention to her emotional needs as well as her physical ones. All babies do best in a secure environment that provides them with an abundance of love.

It is not always easy being a parent, but it is worth making an effort to be patient. Some days may be more challenging than others, but try not to vent your frustration by criticizing your baby or young child unduly, or by making sarcastic remarks. This kind of treatment can be really hurtful to a youngster. It is far better to encourage your baby, so that she grows up to feel at ease with herself.

When a reward is called for, devote special attention to your baby rather than giving her presents or sweets. Babies could not care less about money. At the heart of your baby's development – intellectually, emotionally and even physically – is her relationship with you.

Sharing experiences

Spend as much time as you can doing things with your baby rather than trying to ignore her in order to get on with the things you want or have to do. Have conversations with her about ordinary everyday things and involve her in your life. You may not always have many minutes to spare, so it can be difficult to put

ideals into action. Nevertheless, you can seize opportunities and make the most of time with your baby during daily activities. Feeding, nappy-changing, bathing – even shopping and household chores – can provide chances for one-to-one interaction and stimulation.

Choosing the right activities

The activities you do together should be enjoyable. Babies benefit from some structure to their day, but within that framework it is preferable to be spontaneous rather than impose a rigidly organized programme. Be open-minded and flexible. All babies differ, even identical twins. Take your cue from your baby and follow her moods. She can only learn when she feels receptive. There will be times when she is lively, curious and thirsting for stimulation, and other times when she is not. That is as it should be. She has to recharge her batteries, just as you recharge yours.

Letting go

As your baby grows up, she will change in many ways, not least in becoming more independent from you. It can be a dangerous world, so you have to be aware of hazards and consider her safety at home and outside. But as time passes, your baby also needs to do more on her own, whether it is playing with bricks or learning to dress herself. While your input remains important, it is vital to let her do things on her own. Tempting as it may be, resist the urge to be a 'helicopter parent', hovering over your child all the time.

Finding a happy balance

Most parents are short of time – and none more so than parents who also work outside the home. If you wonder about the effect that working outside the home could have on your baby's progress, bear in mind that that good non-parental childcare has many advantages. Variety of experience enriches a young child's emotional and social

development. It also helps her to learn that she can enjoy herself when you are not there. When you are not at work, spend time with your baby, and rest assured that the concept of 'quality time' really does seem to hold true.

As a working parent, your contribution to your baby's development may be subtly different from that of a parent who is at home full-time, but it is possible to strike a good balance. And, in the long term, seeing that you are fulfilled and successful can spur on your child's own achievements.

Preserving a sense of security

Attempt to protect your baby from the effects of conflict. Emotional stability is hugely important for a developing child, and any threat to her security can have a profound influence on her. If there is disagreement between you and your partner, or other problems in your life, do what you can to shield your baby from it.

bringing out the best in your baby

learning through play

Playing is a thoroughly enjoyable activity, of course, but it is also a serious business. Play is the work of the child, as many educationalists have put it – and that observation is just as valid today as it was back in the 19th century when the educational pioneer Dr Maria Montessori first made it.

Finding out about the world

It is through play that children find out about about their immediate environment and how it works. Playing helps to build a foundation for a child's later learning. Indeed, babies who are deprived of play experiences may even develop

learning difficulties later. Therefore, parents who want their offspring to grow into children who fulfil their academic potential should let them have their fill of playing now.

Play stimulates the senses, especially vision, hearing and touch. It improves babies' powers of observation and helps to develop their coordination and other skills. Through play, a child makes important discoveries about the material world and the laws of nature.

Hands-on experience

Young children learn a great deal more from direct, hands-on experience than from formal teaching, and the younger the child the more obviously this applies. In the 1920s, long before television became commonplace, Jean Piaget, the Swiss doyen of child development, realized that learning had to be interactive, and later studies have shown that children absorb far more from playing than from passively watching a video or DVD programme, for instance (see also pages 128–29).

Toys

Babies need a wide variety of toys of different shapes, sizes, colours and textures. The most complex (and expensive) toys are sometimes the least fun as well as the least helpful for children's development.

Your baby needs to exercise his own imagination, not that of some brilliant toy designer. He will enjoy building towers out of blocks and putting things into boxes. Not all his playthings have to be toys. Sometimes he can have fun with saucepans, empty cardboard boxes and used cotton

PLAY AND COGNITIVE LEARNING

'Cognitive' is a word often used in psychology and child development. Roughly speaking, it means 'related to thinking, understanding, knowing and learning'. A baby's cognitive development is the development of the intellect and the ability to think and reason. These skills sound academic, but they are closely linked to a child's play experiences. In addition to helping your child's sensory and motor skills, play enables him to learn how to pay attention, acquire planning skills, and even to master language. There is good evidence for these claims. They make perfect sense, too, because children, like people of all ages, learn best when they are interested.

Creative play, whether with bricks or finger-paints, helps coordination and stretches the imagination.

reels. He can also do things with you, such as watering your houseplants, that seem like play to him. Some playthings invite your baby to use his imagination more than others, but all toys can be experimented with. An active, enquiring baby often finds new uses for existing toys, and this teaches him a lot about the world.

Books

Books are useful right from the start, and you can read to your baby even before he is six months old. You may not think of ordinary books as interactive, but in this instance the interaction is with you. Your baby will enjoy the rhythm of your voice as well as the bright colours of the pictures, the chance to turn the pages (or try to), and of course the closeness of sitting on your lap.

Types of play

Different varieties of play confer different benefits. Creative play, whether it involves bricks, buckets or finger-paints, helps coordination and stretches the imagination. Your baby will develop a preference for using one hand rather than the other (see pages 106–107). However, using both hands in certain types of play stimulates both sides of the brain, which is important for development.

Active boisterous play helps to release pent-up energies and channel aggression constructively. An outing every day is valuable because it gives structure to the day and staves off boredom. Your baby can experience new things and let off steam at the same time.

Playing with other children

Playing with others helps your baby learn how to socialize, cooperate, take turns and appreciate the existence of rules. A child under the age of 3 may not make any friends as such, but it is still good for his development to meet other babies and to play alongside them.

Role play

Almost any kind of role play is valuable, from playing with a toy telephone to delving into a dressing-up box. This allows a baby to try out different situations and experiment with them in a safe environment. Research even suggests that children that are most imaginative in their make-believe are less vulnerable to stress when they grow up.

Sustained play

Children need to learn how to play in a sustained way rather than constantly flitting from one activity to the next. Sustained play is important for your baby's powers of concentration and his organizational ability. Although he does not recognize it as such, learning to plan-do-and-review is part of sustained play, and is a vital life skill to carry into the school years and beyond. That said, it is just as important not to try to compel your baby to play with something once he has lost interest in it.

learning through play 21

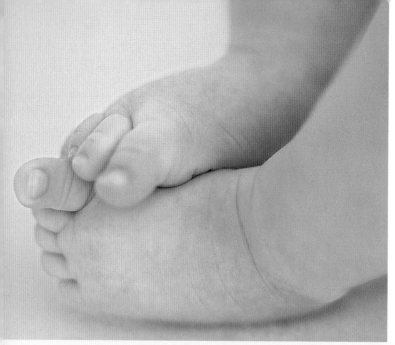
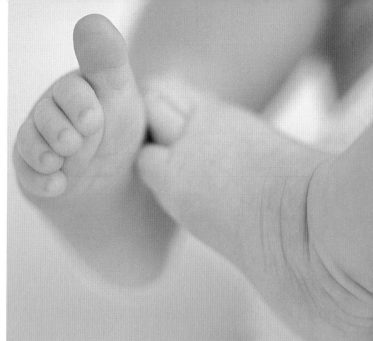

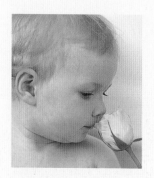

how development works

Parents often think of development in terms of their children passing particular milestones, but in reality growth, whether it is emotional, physical or intellectual, is really a smooth linear process along a path.

Different rates of progress

It is a fact of life that children develop at different rates. Parents are frequently competitive about how fast their child is progressing compared to others, but there is no need to be. Purely physical achievements such as learning to walk may be the most obvious signs of growing up, but they have little connection with a baby's intelligence.

Sometimes, the rate of development runs in the family. For instance, being late in learning how to use a potty can pass from one generation to the next. All the same, babies generally go through each developmental stage in a predetermined order. Your baby will therefore learn to sit before she can stand, and to speak before she can read.

Occasionally, babies skip a stage. Some babies, for instance, never crawl, preferring to get about by creeping, while others favour shuffling on their bottoms (see also page 72).

Link and learn

Every phase of development depends on your baby's brain cells (also called neurones) linking up to form a network. Each neurone can connect with an enormous number of other cells (each junction is called a synapse). Learning means making new connections between neurones.

Whether your baby touches a toy, hears you speak, looks out of the window, smells a flower or tastes a food, each new experience literally leaves a subtle trace on her brain. Repeating an activity reinforces the connections between neurones. That is why practising a new skill makes someone better at making use of that skill.

As your baby's nervous system matures, her nerves acquire a layer of myelin. Part protein, part fat, myelin is a substance that coats each nerve and acts as an insulator, helping to conduct electrical signals faster. At birth, many nerves have no myelin at all. Nerves outside the brain can take up to two years to develop their full complement of myelin, which partly explains why babies have little physical coordination, and why you cannot potty-train your baby until she is about 18 months old. Nerves inside the brain take even longer to develop, and are not fully myelinated until early adulthood, which is one reason why there is no point expecting teenagers to be wholly rational.

Sensitive periods

It follows that babies can acquire a new skill only when they are ready for it. Although there are no rigidly established critical periods of development, there are times when a baby is most ready to master a certain skill. For instance, there is a window of opportunity for learning to chew solid food at around 7–8 months of age. If your baby does not get the opportunity to learn to chew at around this time, then it will be more difficult to do it later, and it could take longer. Learning language is also best done during early childhood. Children who do not learn to speak at the usual time often have lifelong difficulties.

Interrelated skills

Although babies are often considered as acquiring skills in different areas of development, such as movement, language and emotional understanding, the various skills are really interrelated. As a simple example, waving bye-bye means that your baby has mastered the necessary muscle actions in her hand. But it also means that she has reached a particular level of social and emotional maturity. She understands what waving signifies and she appreciates that someone is leaving. That is why development is not simply a matter of your baby doing certain things at certain times. It is just as important to look at how well she does them, and the context in which she chooses to do them too.

Development of the body

Physical development progresses from the head downwards. At birth, your baby's head is the largest part of her body. Her neck muscles develop before the muscles lower down in her back. In the same way, her arms grow in size and strength before her legs. When she is learning to sit up, she will be able to use her hands to play, while her legs are little more than stabilizers to keep her upright.

pre-birth development

Your baby starts life as a single cell only just visible without a microscope. In the next 8 or 9 months, this one cell divides and grows into a full-size baby made up of several thousand billion cells.

The genetic blueprint

Each cell in the human body contains some 35,000 genes. These are your baby's genetic blueprint in the form of DNA, a master code that holds all the information needed for your baby to develop into a complete adult. Babies get half their genes from their mother and half from their father. Since there is a huge number of genes, the number of possible combinations is almost unimaginably massive. A baby's genes therefore make him or her unique.

How your baby's brain develops

The brain and nervous system form from a row of cells along the length of your baby's back when the pregnancy is around three weeks old. These cells rise up in a lengthwise fold, which then makes a cylinder called the neural tube. The neural tube divides into two main parts. The top end becomes your baby's brain, while the rest becomes the spinal cord. His nerve cells multiply quickly, and soon fibres called dendrites extend from each one. The biggest fibre from each nerve cell is called an axon, and its task is to send electrical signals from each nerve cell to the next.

The number of brain cells is almost wholly fixed before birth, and your baby has his full complement by around 20 weeks of pregnancy. But there is more brain development to do. These cells grow in a complex way and many things can affect the process. In fact, your baby has some 200 billion brain cells at birth, which is twice as many as an adult and therefore more than he needs. During development, some brain cells die off. Programmed cell death (called apoptosis) is a normal part of development of many organs. The remaining brain cells make new connections, and this is the way your baby learns (see page 22).

How your baby's limbs and muscles develop

In the womb, your baby's limbs first appear as tiny buds on each side at a few weeks of age. The buds lengthen, enlarge and then grow nodules that eventually become your baby's hands and feet. By 10 weeks or so, your baby starts moving his arms and legs, though you cannot feel it until around 20 weeks. When your baby's nerves develop to the point where they connect up with his muscles, his movements become more purposeful. He kicks his legs, opens and closes his fists and sucks his thumb. He also tries out facial expressions such as frowns and lip movements.

Learning in the womb

Your baby constantly takes little gulps of amniotic fluid, sampling traces of the foods you eat. At birth, his 10,000 or so taste buds are already familiar with your favourite dishes. The fact that a newborn baby is already used to the special taste of his mother's milk probably helps breastfeeding.

Your baby's ears form by 16 weeks of pregnancy, so he can hear from then onwards. He grows used to the sounds of your voice, your heart, your stomach rumblings. Research has shown that babies respond to sounds in the womb and remember them after birth. This applies not only to their mother's voice but also to melodies heard in the womb, such as the signature tunes of television programmes.

Perhaps what your baby hears makes a difference to his long-term learning. There is debate on this issue, with some parents swearing by classical music and its benefits for their unborn baby's brain development. Some mothers even try to make their babies learn numbers before birth, by slapping their bellies rhythmically, but this practice could be annoying as well as pointless.

Toxic damage

Everything that sustains your baby in the womb reaches him through the placenta and umbilical cord – as do any toxins you consume. For example, cigarette smoke contains carbon monoxide and nicotine, among other things, and these pass through the placenta. Carbon monoxide robs a baby of oxygen. Nicotine is a stimulant, and with every puff a mother takes on a cigarette her baby's heart rate soars. Other chemicals in cigarette smoke also affect a baby – for instance, by interfering with the transport of both calcium and protein components across the placenta. It is small wonder that smokers have a 50 per cent higher chance of having a baby with some impairment of brain function.

A heavy intake of alcohol by the mother interferes with the normal movement of cells in a foetus's brain. While few women drink the large quantities that can lead to the permanent facial defects and learning difficulties of fetal alcohol syndrome, many women may drink enough to harm their baby. Around 20 units a week (20 small glasses of wine or 10 pints of ordinary lager) can reduce a baby's IQ by several points. Even 15 units a week can lower a baby's

birth weight or cause miscarriage. So far there is no hard evidence that very low amounts, such as 4 units a week, can harm a baby, but some women prefer to drink no alcohol at all during pregnancy, to be on the safe side.

Nutrition in pregnancy

Your own nutrition is vital throughout pregnancy. It is not just a matter of avoiding foods that might harm your baby, such as soft ripened cheeses that could contain listeria. It is also about making positive choices that will benefit your baby.

For example, essential fatty acids, especially LCPUFAs (long-chain polyunsaturated fatty acids), are needed for healthy development of the brain and eyes. The last three months of pregnancy are the most crucial in terms of LCPUFAs. Vegetable oils (corn oil, sunflower oil, palm oil, rapeseed oil) and evening primrose oil are all rich in omega-6 fatty acids, while fish and soya are rich in omega-3 fatty acids. The body converts these to LCPUFAs, especially DHA (docosahexaenoic acid) and AA (arachidonic acid).

Iron is vital for many brain processes; it is also important to get enough folate, zinc, iodine and protein, among other

Your own nutrition is vital in pregnancy. It is not just a matter of avoiding foods that might cause harm. It is also about making choices to benefit your baby.

things. A balanced diet with a range of fruit and vegetables, meat or pulses helps optimum development. In addition, glucose is a baby's fuel, so it is unwise to diet in pregnancy. Complex carbohydrates like potatoes and other starches supply a steady amount of glucose, so they are better than refined carbohydrates such as cakes and biscuits.

Stress in pregnancy

Centuries ago, a pregnant woman's experiences, and even her thoughts, were believed to affect the well-being of her unborn baby. Now science tells us that this is at least partly true. Stress in pregnancy, for instance, can harm a baby. Severely stressed mothers tend to have children who are hyperactive. The level of the stress hormone cortisol in an unborn child is strongly linked to the level of the hormone in the mother. Stress is also linked with premature and low-birthweight babies – probably because stress reduces blood flow to the womb, and therefore to the placenta and baby. While no one can become calm to order, this suggests that it is worth trying to manage stress and anxiety in pregnancy.

Fetal origins

What happens in the months before birth crucially affects a baby's whole future. This is because an unborn baby can adapt his own development, resetting his system to survive if nutrients run low. But deprived conditions may not last for ever. There is evidence that babies who are poorly nourished in the womb, and therefore lightweight at birth, do badly long-term if they then grow up in an environment with abundant nutrition. That is probably because their system has become poorly equipped to living with plenty.

premature babies

A baby who leaves the womb ahead of schedule misses out on the final maturation time that she would have had in the normal course of events. However, expert medical support combined with your loving handling can work wonders to improve the outcome for a premature baby.

A changing outlook

The duration of a normal full-term pregnancy is around 40 weeks (280 days from the start of the mother's last menstrual period, or 266 days from the fertilization of the egg). A premature baby is any baby who is born before 37 weeks of pregnancy.

In the UK, almost 8 per cent of babies are born too soon. Despite the host of advances in modern medicine, this figure has barely changed in 20 years. What has changed is the outlook for premature babies.

Caring for premature babies

Premature babies have an extra requirement for nourishment, warmth and protection from infection. Some of them need assistance in breathing because they do not yet produce an essential chemical called surfactant, which helps air get into the lungs, so they may have to be put on a ventilator.

If your baby is premature, it is likely that her liver is lacking in enzymes, so she may be jaundiced. In addition, her brain is immature, so doctors often use scans to check how a premature baby's brain is doing.

Since the baby's nervous system is under-developed, her sucking reflex may be weak. This is why feeds sometimes have to be given by a tube that goes up the nose and then down the throat into the stomach. Even then, breast milk is still the best food because it contains valuable white blood cells, nutrients, hormones and growth factors. Premature babies need these, if anything, more than full-term babies.

Importantly, breast milk is rich in the long-chain fatty acids, or LCPUFAs, that are vital for the development of both the brain and eyes (see also page 26). Nowadays, LCPUFAs are added to all pre-term formula milks in the UK, even though it has not yet been proven what benefits they bring to a baby's development. That is why it makes sense to breastfeed if possible, even if you have to express your milk so that your baby receives it by tube.

A special-care unit

At first, it is difficult to develop an attachment to a very tiny, premature or sickly baby. However, even if your baby has been placed in a special-care baby unit, it is good for you to get acquainted with each other. You can do this by taking part in your baby's everyday care, including feeding and nappy-changing. You may need to make a special effort to relate to your baby, and you may need the nurses to show you the practicalities of handling her.

Bonding with your baby

A special-care baby unit is a bewildering place for parents and for babies, but there are some things you can do to make it seem warmer and more natural, and to encourage bonding with your baby. For example, there is now little doubt that singing to babies and playing gentle music can help them to thrive. Indeed, this approach may have its comforting effect by recalling events that occurred before birth. Babies who have been spoken to softly or sung to in the womb have learned to recognize and be soothed by the sound of their mothers' voices.

If her condition allows, lift your baby out of the incubator to hold her. Babies love being held against a parent's chest. Skin-to-skin contact is even better, since it allows your baby to hear, feel and smell you. This kind of contact, also called kangaroo care, can calm your baby's breathing and help her development and growth. Premature babies can also benefit from lying on a sheepskin. Being surrounded by softness, it seems, has an almost magical effect in helping a baby to develop and gain weight more successfully.

Your baby's future

Being born too soon means that a baby starts life at a different point on her growth scale from full-term babies, so she will be lighter and smaller than average. However, premature babies can catch up very quickly (twins seem to catch up the most quickly). Some babies stay on the small side, but unless your baby was extremely small, the chances are that by the age of 2 you will see little difference between your baby and one born at full-term.

In terms of milestones, you can expect a baby who was born two months early, say, to be roughly two months behind the average in her general development. To avoid unfair comparisons, you need to take this into account. But, all being well, this too evens up in time.

Premature babies can benefit from lying on a sheepskin. Being surrounded by softness has an almost magical effect, it seems, in helping a baby to develop and gain weight more successfully.

the new arrival

0–3 months

what is he like?

Parenthood is rarely exactly as anticipated. Whatever you expected your new baby to be like, the chances are that you are in for a few surprises. Getting to know your baby can take many weeks. As you learn to respond to your baby, your baby is in turn learning very fast from you.

The newborn

At birth, your baby is immature and helpless, although not in every respect. He makes his entrance into the world equipped with, for example, a bundle of reflex actions such as sucking and swallowing.

Unlike newborn kittens, whose eyes remain shut for a week, newborn babies are able to see. They can hear too, and they can recognize the sound of their mother's voice. You could say that your baby resembles a powerful new computer just unwrapped from its box, before much software has been loaded onto it. As it happens, babies are far cleverer than any computer because of their enormous capacity for learning. Instead of being limited by the size of its memory, the brain of a human baby has a great deal of plasticity, so it is capable of adapting to changing circumstances. Importantly, your baby alters his learning style as he grows. So, unlike the computer you buy today, he will never need an upgrade.

You and your baby

One of the things that your baby is programmed to do is to cry. He is incapable of coming to fetch you, or even of reaching out for you, let alone telling you what he needs. So, whether it is day or night, he uses his voice. And the

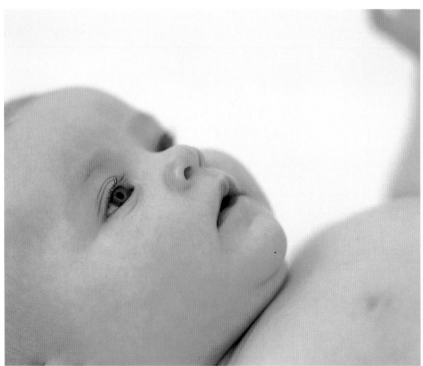

tactic is successful – not least because, as his parent, you are programmed to respond to his cry. This connection between the two of you is very powerful right from the start, and it lies at the heart of your baby's development in every sphere.

As he grows in size and complexity, your baby acquires new skills at an awe-inspiring rate. Every day brings a little something new. You may not always be conscious of these developments on a day-to-day basis since you spend so much time with him. This is a good state of affairs because each moment that you spend together matters.

You are not only the source of his food, warmth and security but also his first teacher. All his attention is focused on you. As he studies you, drinking in your appearance, your taste and your smell, his innate attachment to you deepens. He basks in your warmth and learns all the nuances in your voice. This is a perfect game-plan for his survival and for his learning.

Early reflexes

Your baby's reflexes are automatic responses that have evolved, more or less obviously, from the need for self-preservation. It is thanks to a reflex that your baby sucks any vaguely nipple-like shape put into his mouth. He swallows too, something he could already do while in the womb. He startles if there is a sudden noise or movement. This is also a reflex, just like his blinking and sneezing. A baby automatically sneezes in bright light or if his nose is irritated in any way. In bright light, he blinks to protect his eyes. His body does the right thing without his having to understand what the threat is.

Being involuntary responses, reflexes have clear benefit in protecting him. Some reflexes, such as the strong grasp of your finger if you put it in his palm, are of less obvious value and are simply echoes of our evolutionary past. The early reflexes will fade as your baby's nervous system matures and he learns voluntary movement.

ACHIEVEMENTS AT 3 MONTHS

By 3 months, your baby
- has head control
- can raise his head and take his weight on his arms when lying on his front
- has lost most of his primitive reflexes
- spends time moving his arms and legs
- lies flatter, and no longer holds his arms and legs bent all the time
- begins to stare at his own hands
- can reach towards a moving object

- can grasp a toy placed in his palm
- makes more eye contact
- can recognize faces other than his parents'
- can follow a dangling toy from side to side
- can localize sound
- responds to strangers who are nice to him
- can smile when you speak to him
- can make vowel sounds and a few consonants
- has a variety of different cries
- can produce real tears when he cries
- can show pleasure
- enjoys attention and hugs

holding and handling

Not all babies have the same temperament. Some are placid, while others are much more vocal and demanding. When it comes to handling a newborn, the important thing is to respond to your baby's needs, tailoring your actions to her, not to some idealized picture of how a baby should be.

Holding your baby

Since your baby has little head control for the first eight weeks of life, you must make a point of supporting her head when you handle her. This becomes second nature to you, but you may want to show others how to do it or remind those, such as grandparents, who may be out of practice.

Many parents instinctively hold their baby in their left arm. For right-handers, this obviously leaves the dominant hand free. It may also calm your baby by keeping her close to the reassuring beat of your heart.

Calming your baby

However you hold your baby, take it slowly when picking her up, putting her down or handing her to someone else, even when you are in a hurry. Hasty movements seem threatening and your baby may cry.

An aura of calm and relaxation helps to settle a baby. It is not clear how babies manage to pick up on a parent's mood, but they can. If you are tense, your baby may be too. It can be challenging being a parent, especially if your baby is demanding, so keeping calm at all times is a tall order. However, it is worth making an effort.

Fathers and others

A father's loving handling, while it may be different from a mother's touch, is beneficial to a baby's development. Other adults can contribute too. Getting to know other care-givers will not substitute them for you in your baby's affections, but it can be stimulating for your baby as well as giving you a much-needed break.

Rocking and sleeping

Babies enjoy rocking movements, and a fractious baby may become calmer when rocked or when walked around the room while being held on a parent's shoulder. This may be because it replicates what the baby felt before birth. But avoid rocking your baby to sleep every time. A baby who is always rocked or lulled to sleep in a parent's arms can later become a baby with sleep problems. Your baby has to learn to doze off on her own, so put her in her cot when you think she is tired, whether her eyes are shut or not.

Crying and responding

Naturally you can't always respond immediately to a crying baby, but don't let her cry longer than necessary. A baby whose needs are met grows up secure and in the best position to develop emotionally and intellectually.

Research shows that babies left to cry do not quieten. On the contrary, they cry more. The stress engendered by crying may even have long-term effects on a baby through the production of the stress hormone cortisol. High levels of cortisol in the first few months of life could alter the anatomy and chemistry of the brain in a lasting way. Being left to cry may, it seems, permanently skew development

of the two sides of the brain, increasing the activity of the right half at the expense of the left. So, whenever you can, respond to your baby when she cries, even if it contradicts the advice of previous generations.

BONDING

The term 'bonding' usually refers to the strong rush of affection that a mother has for her baby early on – a transaction that is one way, at least to begin with. Some mothers feel bonded during pregnancy, while others do not until after the birth. A great deal of worry is generated over the issue of bonding, but it does not seem to matter even if strongly positive feelings do not develop for days or even weeks after the baby is born. In fact, there seems to be little link between a mother's bonding with her baby and the development of her baby's long-term attachment to her. So there is rarely any need to get over-anxious about the issue of bonding.

nourishing your baby

Nutrition during the early months of life has a major influence on children's well-being and long-term development. Although breastfeeding a baby is superior to bottle-feeding, each method has its pros and cons. Whether you breastfeed or bottle-feed, you need to be at ease with your decision.

Breastfeeding your baby

Breast milk supplies all the nutrition a baby needs in the first few months and delivers it at the right strength and temperature. It even adapts in quality to a baby's changing needs. Breast milk is not just a blend of proteins, fats and carbohydrates but also a living substance containing antibodies and even white blood cells to help protect babies against infection. For this reason, breastfeeding may also reduce the risk of cot death, but not all studies confirm this. Breastfeeding provides some protection against the

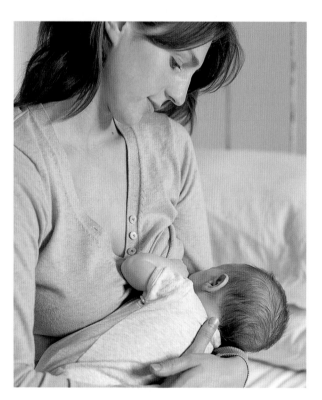

development of allergic diseases later in life, but this is not absolute. Breastfed babies can, and do, develop asthma, eczema and other allergies.

A breastfed baby is less likely to be overfed than one taking formula milk, and breastfed babies are less prone to become overweight or have high blood pressure in adult life. They are also less likely to develop diabetes as children or adults, and in adolescence they are more likely to have healthy cholesterol levels. You may choose to breastfeed for these reasons alone.

Some studies suggest that breastfeeding could lead to better brain and eye development, but they are not conclusive. Overall, the pre-birth environment is probably more important for the development of your child's brainpower than the feeds he gets after he is born.

Using formula milk

Bottle-feeding with infant formula milk has some benefits. For a start, someone else can feed your baby while you work or do something else. Successful bottle-feeding does not depend on your presence or your state of health, and it is not affected by any medication you may have to take.

There have been many innovations in child health, and modern formula milks are now very good when prepared properly. Formula contains more iron and more vitamin D than breast milk. Recently, prebiotics, antioxidants (such as beta-carotene) and long-chain fatty acids, or LCPUFAs, have also been added to some formula milks. Some milks also contain nucleotides to boost the immune system and promote good digestion.

Making the choice

It is difficult to conduct controlled scientific studies into baby feeding, and there are some myths. In terms of your baby's attachment to you, the method of feeding seems to make no difference. Spending time with your baby and caring for him matter much more.

Nobody can really make the decision about breast versus bottle for you. When your baby is very young, you will spend much of your time feeding, so you have to be content with the choice you make and should not feel pressurized into choosing one method or the other. After a few weeks or months, many mothers combine breast and bottle-feeding, and feel that they have the best of both worlds.

Practical matters

A breastfeeding mother needs plenty of protein, iron, calcium and carbohydrates in her diet. There is also a role for essential fatty acids of the omega-3 and omega-6 type, because of the benefit of LCPUFAs on your baby's development (see also page 26). In fact, levels of LCPUFAs in breast milk vary greatly from one woman to another.

Babies are good at regulating their own food intake, but they have erratic appetites at first, which makes it hard to predict what they need when. Whether you use breast or bottle, the best plan is to feed your baby on demand. The main exception is for very premature babies, in which case your paediatrician, family doctor or health visitor will advise you.

Finally, however you feed, take the opportunity to spend unhurried time in gentle one-to-one interaction with your baby. These moments are good for a baby's development, over and above the calorific content of the feed. And they are good for you too. Babies grow up quickly, so savour those precious times together.

Use the opportunity to get close to your baby physically so you can both enjoy the warmth and intimacy of the feed.

feeding his senses

Even at birth, babies are capable of distinguishing between human faces and other sights, and they can tell human voices apart from other sounds in their environment. You can build on what your baby already knows to enrich her experience of learning right from the earliest days.

Even though their colour vision is still immature, babies enjoy bright colours and contrasts.

Visual ability

A newborn baby sees best at a distance of 20–25 cm (8–10 in) from the object of sight. This conveniently happens to be how far away a mother's face is from her baby's at feeding times. At birth, your baby is more interested in looking at faces, or line drawings of faces, than at random patterns. It has even been shown that babies prefer smiling faces to grumpy ones.

Even though their colour vision is still immature, babies enjoy bright colours. They also like contrasts, black and white stripes being a favourite. Your baby does not have a mature sense of perspective yet, but she has some appreciation of distance. She can also follow a bright light or a large moving object for a second or two, if it is at the right distance.

Stimulating vision

In the first two to three months, your baby's eyesight improves immeasurably as her brain makes new connections between nerve cells (see page 24). You can stimulate your baby's development by letting her see the things she most likes, and making sure she can see other interesting things. For instance, she may like to be held on your lap facing outwards sometimes. If she is in a sling, do not block her view of the world.

She can have things to look at in her cot and pram, but avoid clutter. Clutter is distracting to babies and can lead them to lose interest and become detached. She may like a mirror, even though it will be a long time before she appreciates that it is her own reflection on show.

Mobiles suspended from the ceiling help a baby to learn about distance, movement and perspective. Position a mobile so that your baby cannot reach it. Have a variety of brightly coloured

objects. It is preferable to have several different things on the mobile – for example, a variety of animals – rather than simply having different versions of the same animal.

Hearing ability

Your baby's hearing is acute at birth. If she hears loud noises, she will react violently, with a startle, so you must protect her. If she is upset, remember that the sound of your voice is soothing. So is white noise, which you can get on a cassette tape, but it only works if started within two weeks or so of birth. The sound of a vacuum cleaner is similar and can also pacify a baby, though it may not have such a restful effect on you.

Nurturing hearing

Let your baby experience different sounds, including soft music, music boxes and your singing. Keep loud toys away from her. Noise can permanently affect hearing, and the

damage is cumulative. Much of the hearing loss in midlife and beyond is actually noise-induced damage over decades.

Touch and taste

Crammed into your baby's skin are millions of nerve endings that detect touch, pressure, tickle, cold, heat and vibration, so it is not surprising that a baby uses touch as much as her other senses to discover the world. Even at birth, she likes things that are soft. Let her feel your face and your hands, and hold her close to you sometimes when you are naked.

Babies enjoy the feel and taste of their own skin, and many suck their thumbs. This is a normal part of your baby's development, so do not try to stop her. Most dentists now believe that thumb-sucking does not do any permanent damage to teeth.

Developing touch and taste

Your baby needs toys with different textures, to broaden her experiences. Unless the weather is very cold, forget about putting on mittens and bootees, since they can get in the way of sensation. Play with your baby as you talk to her, touching her hands, feet and the rest of her body, varying your touch from a tickle to a firmer feel. You can play games like 'This little piggy' gently from an early age.

Your baby may also enjoy having her legs and tummy splashed in the bath, though you need to hold her securely too. If she does not enjoy splashing, leave it for a while. Whatever you do with your baby, it needs to be at her pace, so take your cue from her.

Synthesizing sensory messages

Your baby will learn to synthesize the messages she gets from different senses. When she looks at a teddy bear, she enjoys exploring its soft texture as well as looking at its face and perhaps chewing on its ear.

Some objects produce a certain sensation when your baby touches them with her hand and a different sensation if they come into contact with her bare skin. You can try gently caressing her arm with a soft toy; the feel of it will be subtly different from the one she usually experiences.

SENSORY OVERLOAD

Too much stimulation can be as bad as too little. If your baby's senses are overloaded, you may notice that she blinks a lot. Or she may turn away. If the stimulation continues, she becomes unhappy and may cry and kick out. When it all gets too much, babies enjoy a quiet undemanding cuddle or even just a sleep. Keep in tune with your baby's moods and her level of alertness.

making the most of movement

At first, your baby lies curled up most of the time – a legacy of his fetal position. Then he discovers that he has room to move and stretch, and during the next few weeks his muscles start to develop and strengthen. By 3 months of age, he will look far straighter, and he will have learned a lot too.

Head, neck and back

Many young babies lie with their head tilted to one side as a consequence of spending so much time on their back (a bald patch on the favoured side is not uncommon). If you add to that a degree of skull asymmetry, it is not difficult to see why babies tend to favour one particular head position.

Although the 'Back to Sleep' campaign recommends that babies should sleep on their back to reduce the risk of cot death, this does not mean that your baby should lie on his back during all his waking hours. It is beneficial for a baby's development, both physically and intellectually, to experience a variety of positions when he is awake.

To help his trunk and neck control, your baby should have some 'tummy time' every day, while you watch over him. Since he will not be able to raise his head at first, he will not want to spend long like this, though you can make it more interesting by putting him on a play-mat or placing a soft toy within easy reach. As the weeks pass, you could arrange a circle of toys around him to encourage him to stretch and to help his muscles develop in all directions.

If your baby dislikes 'tummy time' at first, you can join him on the floor or he can lie on his tummy atop your tummy. Make sure his own belly is not too full when you put him on his front. Incorporating 'tummy time' in a daily routine – by making it the sequel to a nappy change, for instance – can help get babies to accustomed to the experience, and even look forward to it.

Moving around

Your young baby can exercise his arms and legs, but he cannot change his body position on his own. It is up to you to provide the variety of experience that he needs for his development. Limit the length of time he spends in any one pose, be it sitting in a bouncy chair or car seat or lying

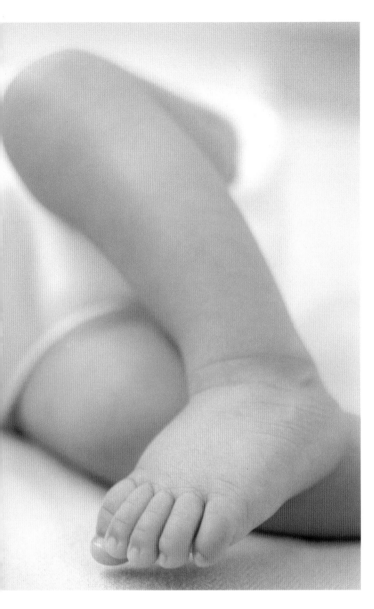

Passive movements

Your baby will also enjoy your playing with his arms and legs, so try gentle passive movements. Lift each arm in turn, and fold it across his chest towards the opposite shoulder. You can also push his legs up in turn gently towards his abdominal area. Although he will make cycling movements on his own, he will experience a different sensation when you do it for him, and he will also get the benefit of eye contact with you at the same time.

Hand–eye coordination

Gradually your baby's fists will become less tightly gripped so that by 12 weeks his hands lie open, ready for the next phase of his learning.

You can help the development of your baby's hand–eye coordination by letting him explore your face. Guide his hand in reaching out and feeling new things, such as a rattle. Do this with both his hands. By the age of 12 weeks, he will be able to grasp an object placed in his palm, but his grip is partly involuntary.

A lopsided head

The problem of a lopsided head is usually minor, but it seems to be getting more common because babies spend so much time in one position. Apart from giving your baby regular 'tummy time', you can help by placing things for him to look at on different sides of the pram, alternating sides from day to day.

You can also place his hanging mobile on alternating sides of his cot. Changing which end of the cot your baby lies his head also helps, because the direction of the light and the orientation of the room both have an effect on your baby's head position.

If you are bottle-feeding, you can also alternate the arm in which your hold your baby from one feed to the next, so that he gets a regular change of position.

awake in a pram, ideally before he gets fed up. If he must stay in one place for long, for instance on a car journey, you could change his head position from time to time, using folded towels as a wedge.

Allow your baby to enjoy movement by playing with him while he sits on your lap. Gentle bouncing games will help him to develop his trunk and limb muscles while feeling safe and secure in your care.

baby massage

Massage is an age-old method of healing and soothing. You may already massage your baby without thinking when you lovingly caress her head, chest or limbs.

The benefits of baby massage

As well as instinctively relying on the reassuring effects of massage, you can also use it in a more purposeful way to benefit your baby. Massage can soothe unsettled babies, help to relieve crying and even ease colic. Premature babies and those with problems such as cerebral palsy respond particularly well.

Massage may work chiefly by reducing tension and stress, and thereby reducing levels of the stress hormones adrenaline and cortisol, which can interfere with concentration and learning. It may also help to develop your baby's coordination. Many people claim that massage also tones the muscles, stimulates the circulation and even boosts the immune system.

Massage can aid bonding between parent and child, and it can help parents with postnatal depression to cope with a demanding baby. All in all, massage can be a peaceful and enjoyable interaction for both of you, and you can continue massaging your baby well beyond the early months.

But massaging does not come naturally to every parent. In the west, many adults are unused to touching other bodies, even those of their own children. In order to benefit from baby massage, some may need to rediscover their more primitive and emotional instincts, the ones that polite society dictates they should repress.

Which oils to use

To reduce skin friction in massage, you need some oil, either baby oil or one of several organic oils. Grapeseed oil, coconut oil and sunflower oil are all good choices. Babies have a tendency to taste massage oil by putting their hands in their mouth, so it is generally advisable not to use aromatherapy oils. Avoid sweet almond and other nut-based oils because of the risk of allergy. You need only a small amount, between 20 and 50 ml. Test the oil you plan to use on a small patch of your baby's skin. Wait 30 minutes to see if there is an adverse reaction. If there are any blotches or weals, do not continue.

How to begin

A good time for a massage is after a bath and before a feed, unless your baby is very hungry. Begin your baby's massage by washing and warming your hands and removing any rings. Make sure the room is warm. You may need a warmer room than usual, about 26°C (79°F), for massage.

More importantly, your baby needs to be contented and warm. Using eye contact, check if your baby is in the mood for a massage. Ideally, your baby should be relaxed and alert. It does not matter if your baby falls asleep during her massage, but you should stop if she does.

Although your touch should always be gentle, especially when your baby is very young, apply light pressure rather than a tickle. There are several basic massage strokes, and you can use a combination, depending on the part of the body that you are massaging.

The open-hand technique involves using your whole hand, palm and fingers, to massage your baby. In closed-hand strokes, your fingers envelop her limbs, which can feel very reassuring to a baby. With finger (or thumb) strokes, massage very carefully to avoid scratching your baby with your fingernails. This technique is good for smaller and more delicate areas such as your baby's palms and soles, though you can also use finger strokes on her back.

You can discover more about baby massage and its benefits by attending classes. Your health visitor may know what is available in your area.

FIRST DO NO HARM

There are few dangers, as long as massage is performed properly, but there are some cautions that you should heed. Avoid massage altogether if your baby:

• is under two weeks old

• has had an immunization in the last 72 hours

• is feverish or unwell

• has a skin infection or any other infection

• is asleep

• becomes upset at any time

Postpone the session if your hands or the room are cold. There is no point making the massage uncomfortable or massaging your baby against her will. If your baby dislikes being undressed, she may enjoy having her feet massaged, in which case you can keep most of her clothes on. This can be a good way of introducing her to the pleasures and benefits of massage.

Making preparations

Lie your baby on her back and undress her on a warm towel. Warm a little of the oil in your hands. Before starting the massage, make sure that your baby is happy and calm.

Feet, legs and trunk

Begin by massaging your baby's feet. Wrap your hands around each foot, then use your thumb to work each sole and stroke your fingers along each of her toes in turn. Work your way up each of her legs with a gentle squeeze of your hand, especially as you reach her calf and thigh. You can work your way up the leg, or down the leg, or you can use a combination of directions. There is no right or wrong direction since each of these has merits.

Stroke her belly fairly lightly – a baby's internal organs are delicate – but try not to tickle her. A circular motion for a minute or so is effective. It is said that a clockwise movement aids digestion, because this is the direction in which matter passes through the digestive system towards the bowels, but this is not critical, so do whichever comes most easily to you, and feel free to change direction.

Massage your baby's chest with a firm, open-handed touch. Her heart and lungs are protected by the ribcage. Use crossover strokes, so that you massage from the shoulder on one side to the shoulder, or ribcage, on the other. Stroking from one side of the trunk to the other may help your baby's coordination. Also massage her chest by moving your hands up and down her chest, working both your hands up and down together, and including the shoulders in your movement. If your baby is happy, spend about a minute or so on her chest.

Arms and shoulders

Massaging each arm separately is usually best, because it allows an active baby the freedom to wave the other arm about happily. Move your hand firmly from shoulder down to fingers. You can do this with just one hand, or you can hold your baby's hand with your other hand. Your baby may dislike having her arm held out straight. If so, then simply massage the areas you can reach, which may just be the outside of the arms. There is no point forcing your baby into a pose that she does not enjoy.

Massage the lower arm and wrist with a wrapping action. Use your thumb to massage each palm, making your strokes into small circles. Again, the direction is immaterial. Use small squeezes of your thumb and fingers to work her fingers. Add more oil as necessary during the massage, but

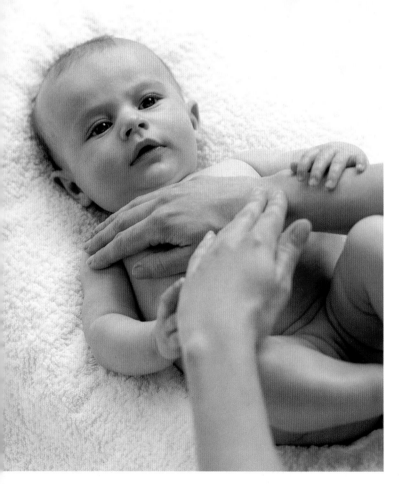

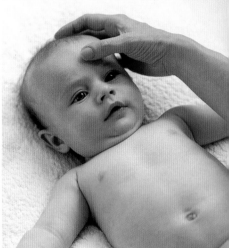

During the massage, keep as much eye contact as you can and smile at your baby. The session should allow you to interact on more than just the level of touch.

remember that your baby is likely to put her fingers into her mouth sooner or later, so she will taste some oil. A relaxed baby will probably let you open and close her arms wide. Gently wrap her arms across her chest and repeat if your baby is still having fun. The stretching motion helps her chest, shoulder and back muscles. She may also find it amusing and reward you with wide smiles.

Head, face and back
Massage her face very gently. To avoid clogging her pores, add no extra oil to your fingers. If your hands are very greasy, wipe them first, and be very careful to keep oil well away from your baby's eyes.

Massage your baby's head gently with open hands, avoiding the soft spot known as the fontanelle. (While babies in fact have two fontanelles in the midline of the skull, the one at the front is more obvious.) You need not bother massaging the back of your baby's head as you would have to lift it up, and she may not like this.

Use your thumbs to massage her face, stroking the nose, chin, cheeks and forehead firmly. You can work both hands at the same time, cradling your baby's head as you do so.

If your baby is enjoying her massage, turn her over gently and massage her back, but avoid the area directly over the spine. You can also massage her arms and legs again while she is lying on her front.

early communication skills

Your voice has special significance for your baby even before birth. Now he picks up extra clues from your tone of voice, your face and your gestures, so he soon understands what you mean. Although he cannot say a word, your baby communicates right from the start, using basic noises and body language.

Smiling

During the first few weeks of your baby's life, you may notice him making fleeting smile-like expressions, probably because he is experimenting with his face muscles.

Only with his first proper smile at about 6 weeks of age does his whole face light up. This is his first real smile and, unlike the brief early smiles, it has emotional significance. Now, when you smile back, his smile gets bigger and delight really shines in his eyes.

Nobody is quite certain why babies first begin to smile. Cheerful expressions on the faces of those around them give them something to imitate, but there must be more to it than that because blind babies can smile too.

Talking to your baby

Your baby can make out meaningful sounds, even in the first few weeks, since the basic ability to learn language is innate. Your baby learns by example too, so he needs you to talk to him. The more you do this, the better it is for his language development. It will be a while before he can reply properly because 'receptive language' (understanding) is always ahead of 'expressive language' (speaking), just as it is when any of us learns a foreign language.

Most parents instinctively use baby-talk, a high-pitched speech with simplified words and lots of repetition. There is a good reason for this. The soft but high-pitched tones appeal to babies and get their attention. More importantly, baby-talk emphasizes certain sounds, so it helps a baby to learn the basics of speech.

Devoting time to your baby

Make time for your baby, even if it means postponing chores. Take every chance you can to communicate on a one-to-one basis, including during nappy changes and bathtimes. Make and maintain eye contact because this is important for conveying meaning. Use your baby's name to encourage him to recognize it from an early age.

Keep background noise to a minimum when you are communicating with your baby. React to the sounds your baby makes and let him have an opportunity to have his say by way of making noises back at you when you have spoken. Sing songs and nursery rhymes to help him learn speech patterns. He will not understand the words yet, but this does not matter.

Talking back to you

Babies learn by imitation from the very beginning. Your baby actually moves his mouth in response to you even when he is just a few days old. Soon he makes his own little noises back at you, often timed to fill the lulls in your speaking. In other words, young as he is, he knows that the art of conversation is about taking turns. When you speak, your baby keeps still to listen. When you stop speaking, he makes sounds and moves his body. If you don't then respond to him, he may become puzzled or upset and he may cry.

As he gets older, his repertoire of sounds grows and he really interacts with you, showing obvious pleasure. His body language too becomes more eloquent. He may curl up or stretch, or use various facial expressions including grimacing and blinking.

Although your baby may have a dummy at night or when he is crying for something but has to wait, it is best for him not to use a dummy during all his waking hours. He needs to be able to experiment with his lips and tongue to develop a full range of speech sounds, so try to avoid giving him a dummy when he does not need it.

YOUR BABY'S FIRST SOUNDS

An infant's first utterances are predominantly vowel sounds such as 'ah', 'eh', 'uh' and 'oh'. Babies generally enjoy making these sounds, especially from the age of 6 weeks onwards. Of all the sounds he can make, your baby may have one or perhaps two favourites. By 3 months, he may have begun to use some consonants. Sounds such as 'g' and 'gn' are mostly happy sounds, while 'b' and 'p' are sounds that he might make when restless or fretful.

getting to grips

3–6 months

what is she like?

The second 3 months of your baby's life will be anything but dull. During this period you will observe her making remarkable strides in her development. She will steadily become bigger and stronger – and, as ever, her physical and intellectual abilities will move forward together.

Hands and fingers

By the age of 6 months your baby's hands lie open most of the time. Indeed, from 12 weeks onwards, she enters a phase of hand regard, when she waves her hands in front of her eyes and studies them closely as if trying to work out what they can do. Before long, she will be making the most of her hands to explore the objects in her immediate environment. Her grasp is clumsy to begin with, of course, but she learns from every experience. Successful actions reinforce the connections between her brain cells.

Your baby's visual ability is becoming steadily more acute and the millions of touch receptors in her delicate skin enable her to feel everything in exquisite detail. Her highly sensitive lips and tongue enhance the experience. As long as she is able to reach an object and it can more or less fit into her mouth, she will pass up few opportunities to make a full assessment of it.

Reaching out

By the time your baby is 6 months old, not only has her reach become more accurate but also she has developed the strength and coordination to manoeuvre her body into new positions. This opens up new possibilities since she can now reach things that were once too far away.

Early social skills

Your baby also starts to reach out socially during these 3 months, discovering who really matters to her. Of the various important people in her world, you are the most important of all. A baby's attachments develop from these early months up until around the age of 4, and depend on the love and security she receives and the special time you spend with her. You do not always have to do something together. Just being with your baby and touching her is beneficial to her comfort and her development.

Responsiveness

Spending time with your baby is fun because she is such delightful company. A baby of this age is very responsive. Although she can't yet talk, her understanding develops, and she learns how to interact in new ways. She makes new sounds, including laughter, and there are also her growing repertoire of body language and her dazzling smiles.

Pacing the days

Even at this tender age, a baby's personality comes through strongly, and she will not feel the same all the time. Expect her actions and behaviour to vary from day to day with her mood. You baby can only learn new things when she is ready, so you need to take your cue from her rather than having a preordained curriculum.

Although variety is the key to enriching your baby's development, and your baby's outlook is subtly different each day, her life nevertheless needs a framework. The timing of the daily ritual of, say, bath, story and bed does not have to be set in stone, but a predictable routine appeals to babies. It enhances their sense of security and can have a calming effect, so it is of emotional benefit. As your baby comes to anticipate pleasurable events, it also helps the development of her memory and even teaches her about different times of day. This is important in establishing a regular sleeping and feeding pattern too.

ACHIEVEMENTS AT 6 MONTHS

By 6 months, your baby
- has excellent head control
- can follow things with her head through 180 degrees
- reaches out accurately
- puts everything in her mouth
- can hold things in her hands, but may drop them accidentally
- is fascinated by detail and small objects
- can wriggle on your lap or in your arms
- can roll from side to side
- can sit with support
- may sit unsupported for a few moments
- holds her arms up in anticipation of being carried
- has a good understanding of different sounds
- chuckles and laughs
- may say 'ba' or 'da'
- is very responsive and sociable
- enjoys listening to people
- is attached to you
- may become anxious when separated from you
- is often fascinated by strangers
- can become shy or anxious with strangers

feeding the senses

At 3 months, your baby is becoming more perceptive, and thanks also to the increasing range of things he can do with his hands, he has many new experiences that stimulate the senses and drive his development.

Interlinked skills

As your baby grows older, his skills in different areas of development become more interlinked. His developing hand–eye coordination helps to bring interesting things closer, so he can feast his senses on them and refine his powers of observation. In this way a world of multimedia experiences opens up to the young child.

Vision

Your baby's near vision is improving, although he cannot see small things well yet. He appreciates board books with simple bright pictures. Mobiles continue to be useful for enhancing his perception of distance and perspective, and you may want to add a new one in different colours to provide fresh stimulation.

Your baby can follow moving objects through a range of 180 degrees, but only if they do not move too fast. You can help to improve his skills by slowly moving something medium-sized, such as a rattle or a brightly coloured ball, across his field of vision.

From now on, your baby can see more distant objects better too, and you can encourage him, for instance by sometimes moving around the room as you speak to him, so that he follows you with his eyes.

Hearing

Your baby is very aware of sounds, including distant ones. He is also better at locating sounds, though even at 6 months he is less good at hearing something immediately behind him.

If you want to use sound to communicate, position yourself for maximum impact. At first, you must make a noise with a rattle or a soft squeaky toy for him, but when his hand skills improve from the age of 4 months onwards, he learns to make them work for himself. Your baby may also enjoy a Velcro wristband with bells on it and a soft ball that chimes when it moves. Such playthings teach him about cause-and-effect too.

Babies enjoy music boxes and other toys that play tunes, but do not leave noisy toys close by your baby all the time. Noise can damage the ears, and the effect is cumulative over a person's lifetime. As your baby cannot yet move away from a toy, or push it aside, his hearing needs to be treated with special respect.

Taste and smell

Many of your baby's experiences involve taste and the closely related sense of smell. At 6 months, if not sooner, he will start to consume solid foods and will have a new world of tastes to sample. Before then, he will sniff and taste many of the other objects within his reach. A dummy can interfere with these sensations, so it is preferable if he does not have one all the time.

Touch

Touch is amazingly important to a baby because it is such an interactive sense and, in addition, it has an emotional component. You can caress and touch your baby directly. Massage continues to be a loving and pleasant sensation

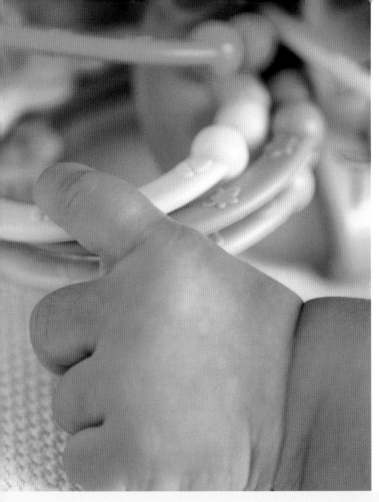

for him, and you can continue this for as long as he enjoys it. Everything your baby touches must be safe, but you can still provide a variety of things for him to experience. Not all toys need to be plastic or furry. He can also have some wooden or fabric toys. You can vary the sensations for him too. Instead of his touching a soft toy, for instance, you can make the soft toy tickle the skin of his leg or arm. This gives almost the same sensation, but not quite.

LINKING AND LEARNING

Your baby progresses by making new links between the nerve cells in his brain, creating a network that is uniquely his. As the months pass, everything he sees, feels, hears, tastes or smells grows more meaningful. Soon, he knows that the high-pitched sound he regularly hears means the cat has entered the room. He has learned to associate the *meow* with the furry face that appears in the doorway. Each new experience builds on what he has learned already, so that, out of the many stimuli that bombard the senses, your baby begins to discern order and significance.

mastering movement

Your baby is not mobile yet, but she is becoming increasingly active, stretching out her limbs as frequently as she can. As a result, her coordination improves all the time. To make the most of her developing hand–eye skills, let her reach out for things, whether it is a toy or your own nose.

Hand–eye coordination

At first, your baby often misjudges distance, and her hand overshoots the object she is trying to reach. But these misses teach her how to do better next time. As well as placing toys for her to reach, you can use finger puppets. Give her positive feedback when she has managed to grasp some new object.

You may notice that your baby grasps using her whole fist at first, but towards 6 months she uses her palm and outer three fingers. Even then, her grasp is still not entirely under her control, and she often drops things by accident. If she holds one toy, she will drop it if you offer her another.

To improve her reach from different positions, have some toys overhead, such as a baby gym, and some below her, such as an activity mat. When she is on your lap, hold out toys for her in different directions, but do not make it too difficult for her to grasp hold of them.

Large motor skills

Your baby is now very active with the rest of her body too. But 'tummy time' is still helpful for strengthening her trunk and arm muscles. You can put toys just out of reach to encourage her to move towards them.

Playing on the floor with your baby is fun for her as well as you. By now, she will be rolling from side to back, and then from back to side. You can help her by lying her on her back and placing a toy out of reach on one side. Bend her knee gently, and help her roll over towards the toy. Soon, she will be able to roll from her back to her tummy. This is a useful prelude to crawling, and shows how strong she has become.

Around the age of 6 months, your baby will learn to sit up. By about 4 months, she can sit if you hold her. As soon as she is happy to sit propped up, arrange some cushions to support her and let her sit for a few moments to enjoy her new upright posture. Soon, you can move around the room. As you watch her, she watches you. This is good for the development of her neck and upper trunk muscles.

Help her balance by playing bouncing games with her on your knee. You can also swing her from side to side, backwards and forwards, as well as round and round, to aid her coordination.

Whenever your baby needs your help in changing position, use your hands to guide her movements rather than doing it all for her. You do not have to lift her and change position for her as you did when she was younger.

Opportunities for action

Your baby may enjoy the occasional larger toy, such as an oversized teddy bear to cuddle. This gives her a chance to use larger muscle groups. She may also like splashing at bath-time. As she approaches 6 months of age, you can bathe her in a big bath. To get her accustomed to it, you could put the baby bath inside the big bath. That way, the high sides seem less daunting, but she can still splash to her heart's content.

Let her reach her feet. She won't need socks or bootees most of the time, and she will move better without them.

PLAYPENS

A playpen can be a good place to play safely, and you can put your baby in it when you need to leave her for a moment, for instance to answer the door or go to the bathroom. However, a playpen can be dull and restricting, even with toys in it. It curtails your baby's exploration and limits her learning. If you use one at all, it should be only for short periods of time. Rotate the toys in the playpen to keep her interested, and take your baby out before she gets too bored.

talking to your baby

Although it will be some time before your baby actually speaks, he communicates by a range of gestures and sounds, some of which even resemble real words. He is also very responsive. Although he smiles at almost everyone, you are the special person in his life, so you get the broadest smiles.

Understanding

Your baby can understand a great deal from your tone of voice, your gestures and your facial expressions. He is able to distinguish almost all the different sounds you make. Although he obviously cannot understand everything you say, he almost certainly understands some words. Research shows that babies pay more attention to sounds that come just before or just after their names, so it makes sense to use your baby's name a lot when talking to him.

Vocal play

During these three months, your baby coos, laughs, babbles and experiments with new sounds. This is called vocal play.

Babies seem to get pleasure from the vibrations they make when they chatter, which may be why they do it even when there is no one listening. During vocal play, your baby learns to associate different sounds with certain lip and tongue movements – an essential skill for learning to speak.

The first speechlike sounds that babies make are single syllables such as 'aw' and 'oh', but you will notice that your baby also uses consonants, and he may repeat syllables to form longer sounds such as 'ba ba ba' and 'da da da'.

From around 4 months, babies make a huge range of more complex sounds such as 'ah goo' and add new consonants such as 'k'. Occasionally they make sounds that are very like real words, but it will be some months yet before they utter their first real word.

Universal sounds

The first sounds that a baby makes are universal, in the sense that these language sounds, also called phonemes, belong to no single language. Language-specific sounds emerge only after the age 6 months or so, as a result of hearing you and other people speak.

Helping your baby's language development

Speak to your baby as much as you can. Baby-talk is useful, as is normal speech. Keep background noise to a minimum so that he can hear you clearly.

Your baby can imitate lip movements, so watching you speak is almost as important as hearing you. Eye contact is especially valuable in ensuring that you maintain your baby's attention and making your words more meaningful.

Make conversation with your baby. Ask questions like 'Do you want me to tickle your tummy?' He will soon know what tickling the tummy means, because he will associate the phrase with the fun he had immediately after you last said it. Leave a pause for him reply. Even though he cannot answer with words, he knows the rules of conversation, and you will be helping him socialize, as well as understand different types of sentence and the rhythms of speech. Similarly, answer your baby when he babbles in your presence.

Read to your baby, and sing songs and nursery rhymes to him. Playing music helps to engage the brain and uses sounds to convey different moods, but keep the volume low and don't have music playing all the time. Too much sound can interfere with a baby's concentration and may even harm intellectual development.

Bilingual households

If you want your baby to grow up speaking more than one language, it is never too early to start. Babies have adaptable brains, especially at the stage when they make universal sounds, and from infancy your baby can easily begin to learn another language alongside the one you consider your native tongue. Many babies grow up in households where two languages are used. This is the surest way of becoming truly bilingual, with excellent accents in both languages.

Some parents, and even a few health professionals, are concerned that a bilingual upbringing can cause difficulties in speaking. However, there is no evidence that babies become confused when exposed to more than one language, or that it delays their learning to talk. Bilingual children speak just as early and just as fluently as other children. For a while during childhood, these children may switch from one language to another when speaking a single sentence, but this does not persist.

sitting up
6–12 months

what is she like?

As she grows, your baby is learning at a staggering rate, and her new physical skills enable her to make important observations. For one thing, sitting upright is now her preferred position. This changes her perception of the world because she now sees it the right way up, just as you do.

New discoveries

Your baby's range of vision improves during the second 6 months of life, so her horizons gradually expand. She touches everything that she can, so she has many new sensory experiences, and she does not miss much of the action around her. She has a thirst for finding things out, and her improved muscle coordination and hand-eye skills mean that she can now make major discoveries about how things work. She learns what happens when she bangs a brick on the table or she touches a prized ornament of yours. As she investigates everything, she is really a mini-scientist, and the world is her laboratory.

Since your baby is not yet fully mobile, you can keep objects out of her grasp fairly easily. However, this also means that you often need to bring within her reach things that are interesting. She still depends on you to enrich her environment and provide her with the stimulation that spurs her development.

New thinking

The connections in your baby's brain are multiplying fast during this period and her brain becomes capable of new ways of working. By 8 months or so, she is able to recognize complex objects in much the same way as an

adult can. Towards the age of 9 months, your baby's new discoveries include important new principles, such as 'object permanence' and 'person permanence'. In other words, she learns that things and people continue to exist even when she cannot see them.

During these 6 months, your baby speaks her first real word. She understands far more than one word, of course. When she does not know the word for something, she knows that pointing to it will get your attention. She needs interaction with you not simply to expand her vocabulary, but to broaden this thinking on every level.

The developing brain

By the time your baby is one year old, her brain will have more than doubled in weight, as compared with its birth weight. At the very front of the brain, the section called the orbito-frontal cortex is developing. This is the part associated with social skills and emotional responses. There is also rapid increase between 6 and 12 months in the number of connections between nerve cells of the pre-frontal cortex, which links different parts of the brain and is important in managing behaviour.

Personality and relationships

Your baby's personality and intellect become more obvious now, as do some of her likes and dislikes. She seems much more like a real little person than a baby.

At the heart of your baby's intellectual and emotional development lies her relationship with you. Since she is such a busy bee, she may need fewer cuddles than she used to. Nevertheless her close attachment is obvious in the way she looks to you for comfort. From around 6 months, she may become distressed if you leave the room and she may try to stop you. When strangers are about, your baby may also be clingy. All this is normal for her age, and a sign that she is developing as expected.

ACHIEVEMENTS AT 12 MONTHS

At 12 months, your baby
- can sit up unsupported
- can play with toys while sitting
- can pull herself up in her cot or with some other support
- can sit down from a standing position
- can get about the room by rolling
- can crawl or creep
- can walk sideways while holding onto furniture
- may be able to walk unaided, or with one hand held
- has an accurate pincer grip
- does not often put things in her mouth
- can now let go of things at will
- may drop things deliberately for you to retrieve
- knows about object and person permanence
- copies your actions
- wants to do many things herself
- can eat finger food
- recognizes many household objects
- understands simple requests and questions
- knows her name well
- says about three words, with appropriate meaning
- is shy with strangers.

nourishing your baby

Food literally fuels your baby's future. What you feed him now will be vital in maintaining his health and development for many years. In addition to sampling foods with different textures and tastes, your baby must also learn to eat in company. Food has an important social role within the family and outside it.

Moving on to solids

Some time around 6 months of age, your baby will need more nourishment than either breast milk or formula alone can give. Just as important, he will be ready for the new experience of eating solid food. He must learn to chew and

swallow, a different process from drinking. These actions help his jaw bone and muscles develop, so they are also important for speech development.

First, his taste buds have to get used to the new foods. Next he learns to help himself, using the newly developed hand–eye skills that make it possible. As with other facets of development, there is a window of opportunity. If your baby stays on milk-only feeds beyond 8 months or so, he may have trouble taking to solid food.

Drinks

Your baby should be learning to drink from a cup by now. A trainer beaker with small holes can help him make the transition. He can have dairy products, but cows' milk should not be his main drink. He should still have breast milk or a follow-on formula milk. To protect his teeth, limit fruit juices (and sweet foods) to mealtimes. The flow of saliva is highest then, so the sugar is more dilute.

Food for the body

Good first foods include baby rice and puréed fruits and vegetables. You can expand the menu to include coarser textured foods, and then try lentils, wheat products, fish, meat, chicken and full-fat dairy products. Finger-foods like toast and fruit chunks are important from about 8 months. Variety is important. Babies fed a limited variety of foods can grow up to develop strong dislikes and even food fads.

Your baby needs the goodness provided by a variety of wholesome meals, but his requirements are subtly different from an adult's. Don't cut back on fat, for example. He needs fats, especially essential fatty acids such as LCPUFAs (long-chain polyunsaturated fatty acids) that are necessary for eye and brain development (see page 26). These are found in many oils, such as sunflower oil, as well as in fish. He also needs enough iron; research shows that around a quarter of toddlers could be deficient in iron. For his bones, he needs calcium and vitamin D. You may want to give him baby vitamin drops containing vitamins A, C and D.

Food for social development

Even early on, try to eat with your baby sometimes. Your example is vital, so avoid taking all your meals as snacks on the run. If he sees you bobbing up and down from the table, you should not be too surprised if, eventually, he does the same given half a chance.

Soon, your baby will sit at the table in his highchair taking part in family meals. He will often be able to enjoy the same food as you, as long as it is low in salt, sugar and spices.

Table manners

Babies are not naturally tidy. Those first few meals of solids will see your baby dribbling food down his chin, putting his hands in the bowl, even applying food to his face and hair. Try not to get annoyed; he is only finding out what the new food feels like.

Your baby will soon want to grab the spoon from you, but he cannot feed himself yet. You can let him have his own spoon to wave about, bash against the highchair or stick in his ear, while you use a second one to ladle food into his mouth.

Preferences

If your baby refuses a particular food, leave it a few days before trying that food again. Or you may find that he takes to something that he has rejected in a different form, for instance mashed instead of in chunks. If he still doesn't like the food, let it be. After all, there are plenty of adults with strong likes and dislikes. There is never any need to force your baby to eat. If you do, you may put him off the whole eating experience. The more laid-back you are about feeding your baby, the better for you both.

feeding the senses

All the senses make an important contribution to your baby's physical and intellectual development. During these 6 months, even the simplest playthings can be the source of a rich sensory experience.

A baby needs a variety of toys to stimulate the senses, but simple toys will do. Presented with two building blocks, she may pick one up in each hand to hold them side by side, as if evaluating them. Shape-sorters encourage her to make comparisons of size and shape.

Improvised toys such as saucepans, baskets, yoghurt pots and wooden spoons are good too. You can also get her interested in more ephemeral things, such as blowing bubbles and lathering soap at bathtime.

Hand control and touch

Your baby's grasp grows increasingly sophisticated. From 8 months or so, she does what humans are designed to do: use thumb and index finger as a pincer to pick up objects rather than grab with the whole hand. This enhances her learning, because she can manipulate things to study them in fine detail, and often rotate them in her hand to observe them from every angle. Sometimes she prods things with her index too. She will enjoy not only toys but also, for example, keys, buttons, and peas on her plate. The sensory feedback helps her to refine her movements next time.

Exploring her body

Around now, your baby may spend a lot of time pulling her ears, chewing her hands, even sucking her feet. Her mouth can feel her toes, and vice versa, so her senses get a double delight. Exploring her own body in this way allows her to build up a mental map of her physical self.

Visual discrimination

Your baby's eyesight is improving, but she still has a long way to go before her vision is as good as an adult's. In the

Multi-sensory play

At around 6 months of age, when your baby encounters a new object, she looks at it, touches it, smells it, tastes it, and frequently drops it or bashes it against something. She is interested not only in the size and weight of the items in her environment, but also their colour, temperature, texture and hardness, and whether or not they make a noise. Her fingers are sensitive, and her mouth is even more closely packed with sensory nerve endings, so it does more than simply taste. In this way, your baby explores the properties of all the things she can reach.

In early childhood, learning is a hands-on experience and all the senses contribute something. When infants use more than one sense to investigate an object, they remember it far better than if they had just looked at it. You may prefer your baby not to touch everything and not to slobber over the handle of your bag, but she learns from these activities.

first few months, the number of links between nerve cells in a baby's brain grows rapidly, peaking at around 9 months, and this is important in enhancing her visual perception.

You can develop your baby's powers of observation by looking at pictures in books with her. Simple tray jigsaw puzzles also aid her sensory development and improve her hand–eye coordination. At first she will barely manage the easiest puzzle, but show her what to do and she will get the idea. As she grows more adept, and her perception improves, she will need no more than a hint from you as to where a piece should go. However, infants differ a lot in their ability to do jigsaws, so try not to expect too much.

Your baby can follow a moving toy and she is increasingly interested in making things move herself. This is a good time for playing with small-wheeled toys (as long as they are the kind that are safe for her age). She will also enjoy rolling a ball around, especially if it chimes as well. Toys that right themselves when pushed over appeal as well.

Object permanence

A baby's first grip is not wholly voluntary, and she cannot release things at will, but from around 9 months she can let go of an object in her hand when she wants to. In so doing, she will eventually find out about gravity and weight.

Before 6 months, your baby does not look for an object that falls out of sight, but by 8 or 9 months she does. This is because she discovers object permanence. The concept may seem obvious to an adult, but it is a significant issue that once occupied the minds of leading philosophers. Understanding object permanence is a sign of your baby's intellectual maturity and a marker of her memory too. Now she is able to find a toy that you showed her before covering it up with a blanket or under a cushion.

From then on, you can play simple versions of games like hide-and-seek, which may make her chuckle or even dissolve into fits of laughter. You need to be sensitive, however, since babies get frustrated if things become too challenging.

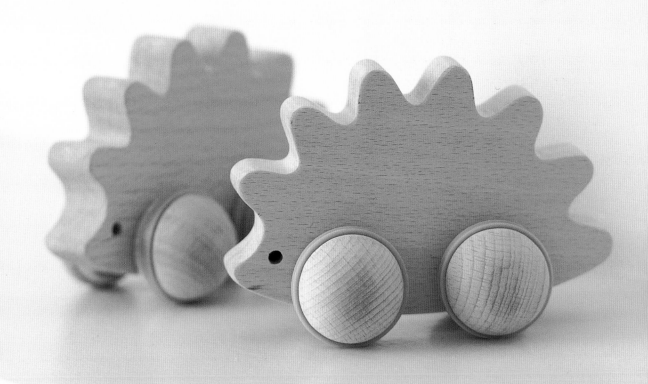

As well as toys, she will enjoy playing with your keys, buttons on clothes, and peas on her plate. The sensory feedback will help her to refine her movements next time.

Cause and effect

Your baby's improved powers of manipulation mean that this is a good time to introduce simple toys that can be made to do something – and in this way your baby can have fun learning about cause and effect.

Even the most ordinary event can teach her something. If she pushes a ball, she sees that it rolls away. If she pushes harder, it rolls further. Your baby gradually learns that greater force has a greater effect. There is a mathematical way of expressing this, but your baby is many years away from learning the equation.

Activity centres, music boxes, toys with buttons to push or levers to press are all popular around now. Versions of many lever-operated toys are suitable for the bath, which is a favourite place for many babies of this age.

Toy musical instruments such as drums and xylophones may appeal too, and can also teach your baby about cause and effect, though her efforts are unlikely to be melodious to anyone but herself.

Stimulating games

Simple activities can stimulate your baby's senses and help her to develop good coordination. 'Where is . . . ? can be a good way to refine her powers of observation and to encourage her to pick things up. However, you cannot expect her to help tidy away toys yet. In a similar vein, you can play 'Give it to me, please,' in which you and your baby hand toys or other small objects back and forth between other. Thanking her makes her feel good and has the added advantage of teaching the elements of good manners.

Using finger puppets with your baby is fun, and can be useful to while away the time when you are waiting, for instance on a train or plane, or in a waiting-room. Puppets exercise the imagination and stimulate the senses, while still encouraging your baby to stay seated.

Play pat-a-cake and clapping games. The rhythmic movements are good for your baby's coordination.

Playing peek-a-boo often enchants babies and it also enhances memory and concentration.

Paper and crayons

Your baby will enjoy crumpling paper and may even try to scribble on it. She is not yet ready for pencils or proper crayons, so give her the short stubby kind. Drawing is still a long way off, but she may enjoy making a few random marks on the paper. She may also tear the paper or poke her crayon through it, but all this has educational value.

Playing on her own

While most of the time your baby will want to play with you, there will be plenty of times when she busies herself happily with toys or by investigating things. As long as you are nearby, she feels safe. It is good for her to play on her own, as it helps to enhance her attention span and powers of concentration. Keep out enough toys to entertain her, but not so many that they clutter the floor and distract her.

mastering movement

In the second half of your baby's first year, his muscles become stronger and his balance improves. He enters an extremely active phase, rarely staying in the same position for long. Some of this movement may seem superfluous, but it is fun for your baby and helps him to work on his muscle control.

Rolling, creeping and crawling

With the help of his hands, your baby will learn to roll from back to front, and from front to back. He may roll around the room in this fashion.

Before long, he learns to heave himself forwards with his hands when lying on his front. By 8 months, he can creep along commando-style and propel himself quite a distance. By about 9 months, he makes more use of his legs and lifts his belly off the floor. Early attempts to crawl are often backwards, but he soon crawls forwards.

Fluent movements

Fluency of movement is as important as speed. Before his first birthday, he should be able to move easily from sitting to crawling and back again. Encourage him by beckoning him towards you, and by positioning toys so that he has to make an effort to get to them. Many babies like crawling though a large play tunnel. You can also offer large cardboard boxes, open at both ends. Make sure that his clothes are crawl-friendly. You don't want him to trip up on loose garments, or have to worry about get nice things dirty.

Before his first birthday, he should be able to move easily from sitting to crawling and back again. Encourage him by beckoning him towards you, and by positioning toys so that he has to make a bit of an effort to get to them.

Sitting

By about 6 months of age, your baby will be able to sit unsupported and before long he can play with a toy on the floor in front of him. By 8 or 9 months, he can sway back and forth, and from side to side, without falling. He reaches forwards for toys and he can combine sitting and rolling. You can help him to gain confidence by rolling a ball on the floor towards him. Your baby will also enjoy moving about in the bath while seated, but keep a hand on him to steady him while he plays.

Standing

Your baby is likely to pull himself into a standing position by about 9 months, using whatever support is handy. At first, he will find it difficult to sit down again unaided, so you may have to come to his rescue. By the time he is 11 months old, he will probably be able to transfer from standing to sitting whenever he wants.

You can help his balance and strength in standing by bouncing him upright on his feet while holding his trunk or his arms. He may enjoy listening to nursery rhymes, or just something you made up, at the same time.

Cruising and walking

By about 10 months, many babies have learned how to walk sideways while clinging onto various forms of support around a room – an activity known as 'furniture-cruising'. From now on, they can mix and match crawling and furniture-cruising to get themselves from place to place.

Before he has learned to walk unaided, and for some time afterwards, your baby may like to have a trolley with bricks that he can push around to give himself stability and fun.

Creeping and bottom-shuffling

Some babies never crawl. Many of them continue to creep commando-style, while others elect to shuffle forwards on their bottoms. However your baby chooses to move, it is a fair bet that he will put on a turn of speed.

A few babies continue to bottom-shuffle for many months and some of them are late walkers. The average age at which a baby walks is 13 months, but walking can be as late as 2 years in persistent bottom-shufflers. This does not seem to matter in the long term, but check with your family doctor if your baby does not walk by 18 months or if you have other concerns about his movements.

Encouraging movement

Mishaps can injure a baby and seriously dent his confidence in his new skills. To avoid them, take time to eliminate dangling tablecloths and flimsy objects that your baby might use as a support. During most of this stage, your baby does not need shoes. His stability depends on being able to feel, so bare feet are ideal as long as he is not cold.

Swimming

From 6 months, your baby may enjoy an occasional trip to the local swimming pool. He is too young to swim but he will like feeling buoyant in the water and he can move around in new ways. To be safe, hold him all the time, even with a flotation aid. He will probably want you close by anyway. If he is afraid of water, do not force him, since it would be counterproductive. Find out which swimming pools have a special parent and baby session. It is easier for a baby to gain confidence in water when it is warm and when there aren't older children jumping about.

talking with your baby

Some time during these 6 months, your baby will say her first real word. Although it may happen one day out of the blue, she builds up to it gradually by studying what she hears and by practising sounds.

Early communication

There is an innate human drive to speak, but to learn to use speech properly a baby needs some intelligence and understanding of the world, and the example of others talking around her. That is why it is vital to encourage your baby to communicate.

Language is more than just the spoken word. One definition is 'a set of symbols to communicate thought'. Language therefore includes reading and writing, but, since babies clearly learn to talk before they read, speech is the first sign of a baby's language abilities. Interestingly, babies who are spoken to a lot often become good readers as well as good talkers.

Understanding

Learning language comes in two stages: understanding others and producing sounds. A 6-month-old can understand much of what you say and by 9 months she clearly responds to her name. She recognizes the words for some 20 or so common objects and may get excited when you mention her favourites. She shows that she understands some of your questions, and by 11 months she may kiss you if you ask her to.

Body language

Around now, your baby uses a lot of body language, just as adults do when trying to speak a foreign language. She may show you things or share them, and these actions are like conversations. Your baby wants you to talk to her, often about the thing she is offering you. Sometimes she likes to hand toys back and forth to you, in a kind of dialogue. When she wants something, or sometimes just when she does not know the name for it, she points urgently and may grunt to get your attention. Developmental psychologists sometimes call this 'referential looking'. You reply, 'Yes, that is a bicycle,' and so extend both her understanding and her vocabulary.

Encouraging your baby's language skills

Provide your baby with a loving and interesting environment. Babies do not require constant stimulation, but they do need speech and interaction.

Take every chance you can to talk to your baby, making eye contact and using her name frequently. Use simple sentences and try to match your actions to your words. Baby-talk is still fine, but do not use it all the time, since your baby has to learn normal speech.

Leave pauses for your baby to reply. Always respond to your baby when she initiates communication by pointing, making sounds or offering you a toy. Say 'please' and 'thank you' when handing things back and forth. This shows your appreciation and teaches her basic manners.

Nursery rhymes, finger games and simple songs all boost your baby's concentration and listening skills. Reading to your baby broadens her understanding and helps instil an early appreciation of books.

First words

Before they speak, babies use their long-term memory to store the words they hear. This process begins in earnest at around 6 to 8 months, when a baby learns the speech sounds of your native language.

As your baby tries out various sounds, her vocal play becomes more sophisticated and can resemble real conversation in its pitch and rhythm. From about 8 months, your baby copies many of the sounds you make, and says a mixture of one-syllable and two-syllable sounds.

At 9 or 10 months, your baby makes her first word. It could be 'da' or 'da-da', even if her mother is her main carer, because 'da' is an easier sound for babies than 'ma'. Your baby has probably said 'da' for some time, but now she says it more when her father is there. By 12 months, your baby makes several distinct words, and some babies even make short sentences. Girls tend to speak earlier than boys, but there is a great deal of variation. Particularly early or late speech development can run in families.

learning social skills

At 6 months, your baby already shows signs of real attachment to you. Forming attachments to others happens mostly between the ages of 6 months and 4 years. Babies grow attached to those who spend time looking after them, and they can become attached to several people.

Attachment to others

The person to whom a baby is first attached is usually his mother but it does not have to be. Forming an attachment does not depend on who feeds the baby or how he is fed. Many babies become attached to their mother first, then their father, and often later to a grandparent or a childminder. Research shows that, contrary to the fears of many working parents, becoming attached to a carer such as a childminder does not weaken the attachment to the mother or father.

Permanence and separation

Babies over 6 months old learn about 'person permanence' – in other words, that someone continues to exist even when he or she is no longer in the room. By 8 months, your baby has a mental picture of the important people in his life. This is vital for attachment and for his future independence as a separate being.

From around 6 months, your baby might play happily on his own, but he may become anxious if you leave the room. He could try to follow you or he may cry long and loud. At times he may be very clingy, especially if he is tired or his routine changes. Parents worry about such behaviour, but it is a normal phase in development and a sign that their baby is attached to them. That is why you need to say goodbye when you leave, and even say when you will be back. He does not yet understand what 'in an hour' means, but he will soon. For now, it matters only that you are not leaving for ever.

Expressing emotion

By the time he is one year old, your baby knows how to wave bye-bye, and enjoys doing this to his favourite people. His sense of fun, like is other emotions, is now obvious. He chuckles when you tickle him, play peek-a-boo or use the wrong words in nursery rhymes. He enjoys dropping things for you to retrieve. Your reactions are important to him, and if what he does amuses you, he does it again and again.

Strangers

Babies are usually shy with strangers at around 6 months. This lessens by about one year, though your baby may still want you close if strangers are about. He may be less clingy, but your presence is still important and he may need to know where you are. That is why at toddler group he may crawl off to play but is less happy if you leave his side.

Other babies

From around 9 months, babies often enjoy being together, even though they are too young to share or to play with one another. You can help your baby's social development

by ensuring that he meets other babies and children. As a general rule, girls are more outgoing than boys and more interested in other people. They notice other people's faces and even their feelings. If you have a boy, however, it is good to help him to read other people's emotions. Even at this age, you can begin to talk in simple terms about different situations and how others react.

COMFORT OBJECTS

Most babies have a favourite soft toy or blanket that they hold when falling asleep or at times of distress. A comfort object helps your baby to face separation from you and is therefore a sign of his attachment to you. As your baby grows up, he loses interest in the threadbare doggie or the scrap of cloth that he took everywhere. This too is normal but, until then, you may want to acquire two identical comfort objects in case one gets lost.

on the go
12–18 months

what is he like?

Your baby is changing fast. In these 6 months, he begins to walk on his own. This skill leads him to make new discoveries. An active toddler can be a challenge to look after, but rest assured that he is using his mobility to enhance his intellectual development. He stands literally on the threshold of great things.

Physical changes

Once your baby has mastered the art of walking, he will soon be toddling everywhere, erratically at first, then much more steadily and confidently. Thanks to improving hand–eye coordination, he is now able to throw a ball, and sometimes even catch one, and he can build increasingly complex structures with bricks. Slimmer and more upright, your little one is now more of a toddler than a baby.

Doing more and more

The outward changes are matched by new developments in your toddler's intellect. He can concentrate far better, so he learns to play in a sustained way, and can therefore develop his skills further. Sometimes he is too engrossed in his activities to notice you, but, when he pays attention, he does not miss much. Highly observant, he watches you closely and mimics much of what you do. He uses this in imaginative play and towards 18 months he begins to develop a rich fantasy life.

Your child's acute senses mean that he learns how to anticipate. Before long, he knows what to do. When you dress him, he holds out an arm or a foot. Although there is still a long way to go until your toddler is independent, this is the beginning of learning to care for himself.

Seeing and discovering

Your toddler's new mobility enables him to explore new objects and try out new experiences. Since he is curious and independent, these are not always the things that you want him to investigate. A determined toddler can move at speed, and there can be hazards along the way, so safety becomes one of your major concerns.

There is no such thing as a perfectly childproof room, and if there were it would be very boring indeed. The ideal is to make his environment safe without restricting his opportunities for exploration and discovery. In practice, this means supervising him closely.

Understanding of others

Possibly your child's greatest feat during this time is his understanding of others. By his first birthday, he starts to appreciate that other people don't necessarily think the same way that he does. Although he is still egocentric, there is now space in his thinking for other people's point of view, at least some of the time. His vocabulary expands rapidly now too, which enhances his thinking. He also develops a grasp of time. His understanding of words like 'now', 'later', 'before' and 'after' is an important advance in structuring his thoughts and memories. All in all, this is a really interesting stage of development, full of possibility.

ACHIEVEMENTS AT 18 MONTHS

By 18 months, your toddler
- can walk steadily
- can walk backwards too
- can bend down to pick up toys
- learns to manage stairs
- can make a tower of three bricks
- embarks on a creative and imaginative period
- can turn the pages of a book
- can see small detail in pictures and objects
- holds a pencil with his fist
- can scribble fluently
- can throw a ball
- can sometimes catch
- is very inquisitive
- is a great imitator
- can point to pictures of familiar things
- enjoys fitting things together
- engages in pretend play
- may feed himself a whole meal
- may try to climb out of his cot
- can remove his shoes and socks
- holds out his arm for a sleeve
- knows his own name
- knows many parts of the body
- understands what most adults say
- begins to understand the concept of opposites
- has some concept of time
- has long conversations with himself
- says an average of 40 words
- may make two-word sentences
- may have a favourite word or phrase
- shows growing independence
- may recognize himself in a mirror
- may play with other children
- may start to have occasional tantrums

feeding the senses

Your baby is a busy bee, exploring the world around her. She is visually very aware and curious to see and do more. This constant activity brings new things into her life, some puzzling, some delightful, and many utterly engrossing. In this period, her knowledge and understanding advance by leaps and bounds.

Fine detail

Your baby now becomes fascinated by small details, such as the pattern on a rug or a crumb of food on her sleeve. You might like to keep a 'discovery box' full of oddments, such as scraps of fabric, a comb, one or two coins, a magnet and the like, to stimulate her senses on a rainy day.

By the time they are a year old, babies understand size, distance and perspective, but their spatial orientation is still immature. That is why your baby sometimes places jigsaw pieces the wrong way up and is unable to see why they will not fit. Tactful clues are usually better than doing it for her.

Scientific properties and concepts

Your baby's avid observations of the world around her enable her to make important discoveries for herself, such as the effect of gravity, the stability of various objects and the strength of materials. In doing so, she may use objects

in ways that are completely different from those intended. Such experimentation is normal and healthy, even when it is maddening to parents. Through experience, young children come to comprehend that materials like water, sand and modelling clay have special properties. You can extend their learning by using words such as 'soft', 'smooth', 'wet', 'runny', 'sticky', 'gritty' and so on.

Playing with sand and with dough exercises your child's imagination. Since they require both hands, these activities have a special value in stimulating both hemispheres of the brain, which aids development (see also page 117).

The beginnings of mathematics

Your baby take pleasure from putting things together. She can enjoy doing simple puzzles, threading beads and placing rings over a post. Again, not everything will be put to the manufacturer's intended use, but this is one way in which a baby makes comparisons. A brick that fits in the gap behind the radiator must be smaller than one that does not. Soon your baby learns about 'bigger' and 'smaller', and about 'less' and 'more'. These basic comparisons are key concepts that help children to tackle mathematics.

At the same time, your baby is learning to put things into categories, another early mathematical skill. She knows the difference between tables and chairs, dogs and cats, and so on. Every so often, however, she is stumped – for instance, by a small square table that could be a stool.

Intensely observant, your baby seeks patterns in things and makes connections. She may begin to arrange bricks on the floor in a certain way that pleases her.

Constructing and deconstructing

The young are great imitators, and your baby will start to mimic your brushing your hair or using a computer. From now on, she can play 'pretend', which occupies her happily and makes her feel big. Planning becomes part of her activities. Towards 18 months, her play can become highly imaginative, and she may create a rich fantasy woven around something as simple as a toy tea set or telephone.

Play with her when required, because this benefits her social skills. She can make quite complicated things with building blocks when she feels like it. However, even when she is more negative and knocks down the towers that you build, she learns something about their construction.

Your baby also scribbles fluently at this age, enjoying making marks on paper. Let her have plenty of it, along with short stubby crayons that she can easily hold in her fist. As always, your appreciation spurs her progress.

Widening horizons

Broaden your baby's range of experience with outings. Visiting the zoo will probably excite her, and you can talk about the sounds and smells as well as the sights.

Even a trip to the local park is a source of stimulation, offering the prospect of going on the swings, playing with conkers, finding an unusual leaf, messing about with a ball or just watching people. Point out things of interest, such as people waiting for a bus or a cat sunning itself on a ledge. You can also mention other senses, for instance the feel of a warm breeze on bare arms.

At around this age many young children start to enjoy water, be it while playing in a paddling pool in the back garden, dipping their toes in the sea on a trip to the beach, or even just splashing in puddles on a wet day.

Books can widen a baby's experience further and show her things that are not part of your everyday life.

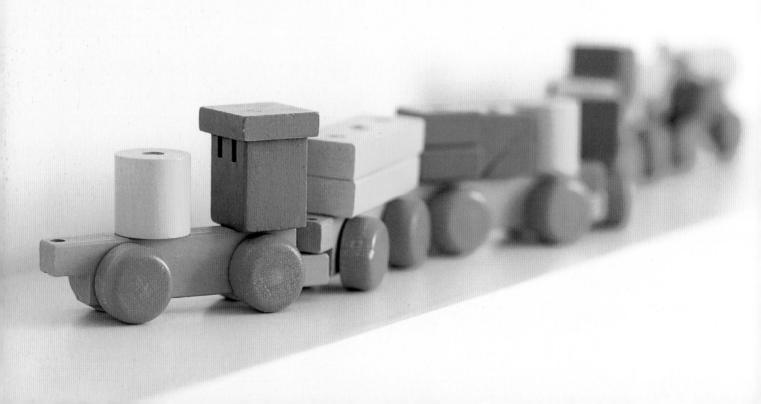

mastering movement

By the time your baby reaches 18 months of age, he will probably be walking on his own. Parents can be competitive about this achievement, though it has little bearing on intellectual development. Babies take that impressive first step at the right time for them, not when mothers or fathers want them to.

Becoming a toddler

By his first birthday, your baby may be walking – or he may still be mainly furniture-cruising and crawling from one place to another. The average age at which a baby walks unaided is 13 months, so if your baby doesn't walk quite yet, he will soon – and in so doing he makes the leap from baby to toddler.

It is actually of minimal importance how babies get about. The crucial thing is for them to be mobile by whatever method they choose, so they can explore their environment to the full and continue their thrilling voyage of discovery.

Doing it at his own pace

From around the age of 12 months, many babies enjoy walking with one hand held, but do not force your child to do this because it may hurt his arm. Besides, pushing him to do something he dislikes, or is not ready for, will discourage him and set his development back. Children walk when they are ready, and there is a wide range of normality.

See your doctor if your baby is not walking by 18 months, however, since very occasionally there can be muscle problems.

The first few steps

One day, probably without warning, your baby will stand alone before taking his first few faltering steps. He will holds his arms high, with elbows bent, to give him greater stability. Although he may not

It is of little importance how babies get about. The crucial thing is for them to be mobile by whatever method they choose, so they can explore their environment to the full.

walk unaided again for a few days, he soon will. As he toddles, his feet will be wide apart, and his steps will be hesitant as well as random in length and direction.

What you can do to help

You can help your baby to overcome the challenge of walking by making your home as safe as possible for him to explore. Highly polished floors, loose rugs and cluttered floors are obstacles for novice walkers.

Your baby needs shoes only when he starts to walk, although he can often go barefoot in the house, which helps his steadiness. If it is too cold for bare feet, he can wear slipper-socks or bootees. Unless your home is fully carpeted, non-slip soles are a must.

For walking outside, he needs proper shoes, which are best bought from a children's shoe shop where he can be expertly fitted. His shoes do not have to be supportive, but they must fit well and be comfortable. Soft shoes are frequently better because they allow a toddler greater sensation, which will make it easier for him to master walking.

Perfecting balance

Once walking, a baby quickly learns to balance. Before then, as well as afterwards, you can help with bouncing games on your knees. Clapping games and rhymes aid his sense of rhythm and also help his coordination.

Mothers and fathers tend to handle babies in different ways, with mothers being more gentle and fathers more physical. This variety is good for a baby emotionally and also helps to develop his balance skills.

By 15 months, your toddler will probably be walking well, and no longer needs to hold his arms aloft, but he will still takes a tumble now and again, so supervise him closely.

If you have stairs at home, use a stair gate whenever you are not watching closely. From around the age of 15–16 months, your toddler may cope with stairs by going up on all fours, and coming down by sliding on his tummy or on his bottom. By 18 months, he may still go upstairs on all fours, or upright on two feet, with two feet per step.

Outside, he needs to have his hand held for his safety. Not all toddlers like this, and reins can be a better option, allowing a toddler the freedom to get to grips with the world with both hands.

Many parents and carers continue to use a buggy for a child long after he has learned to walk. It is difficult to guess how far a new walker can manage; and the distance a toddler is keen to cover can vary from day to day, according to his mood. Sometime a folded buggy is handy to have on an outing in case toddler tiredness sets in.

THROWING AND CATCHING

Although parents tend to put emphasis on walking, because it is such an obvious milestone, there are other important measures of a baby's mastery of his large muscles. Dropping things for you to retrieve is a favourite baby pastime at around the age of 12 months, though by 18 months it should be losing its appeal. From about 15 months of age, a baby can often let things go in an intended direction. Let him attempt to throw or roll a ball towards you. At this stage, his catching is also rudimentary. Unless you sit on the floor very close by, he will be discouraged by his lack of power and poor aim. As his skill improves, you can gradually move further away. Requiring only one ball between you, this simple game helps to develop his ball skills as well as his hand–eye coordination and his balance.

learning language

Your one-year-old is responsive when you talk to her. She knows the names of many everyday objects and by 18 months she knows parts of the body. She understands questions such as 'Where is the cat?'.

Making words, making sense

An average one-year-old says three words with meaning. She also babbles, using a mix of real words and her own sounds. She may have long conversations with herself, or with you, using words, jargon, facial expressions and body language. At times, she may sing, more or less tunefully.

By 15 months, she repeats most words that she hears, so it is no wonder that her vocabulary increases every day or two. Around now, she may say six words, including some two-syllable sounds, or she may say many more.

By 18 months, she is likely to speak about 40 words, but she may not use them all correctly; many toddlers use 'Dada' to mean all men, for example. She knows her name and is likely to refer to herself in the third person. She does not use pronouns, though she understands them when you do.

Her pronunciation is immature, and some sounds, such as 'p', 'b' and 'm', she finds easier than others. Consonant combinations are especially hard, so she says 'dink' instead of 'drink'. Even so, most adults should understand her speech most of the time, although you will understand her best.

Many toddlers start putting words together in simple sentences by around 18 months, using forms like 'Dada gone'. Your toddler may develop her own favourite phrase, using it often. One favourite word or phrase could mean many different things. These are sometimes known as holophrases. Her use of, say, 'mik' to refer to both 'milk' and 'juice' does not mean she cannot tell the difference.

Stimulating language development

The most important thing you can do for your toddler is to talk to her. Make time for conversation together despite your busy life. Make eye contact when you speak, and use her name. Also name things that you see about you, and talk about them. Even ordinary things and events are important to your toddler. You may find the rain an irritant, or the doorbell an annoyance at 7am, but she may well be fascinated, so make the most of everyday experiences.

Name colours for your toddler to learn, but do not worry if at first she mixes some of them up. Help her to recognize groups of things, like shoes, dogs, cups and so on. Help her to learn body parts by using rhymes, and by naming them with her, for instance when dressing and undressing. Repetition helps her to learn. Picture books can extend her knowledge and test her recognition of things.

Nursery rhymes and simple questions

Teach her nursery rhymes. The words and sound patterns help to extend a toddler's language skills. Every so often, you can substitute a different word. She will notice, and probably laugh, if you say, 'Round and round the garden like a huge pink pig' (instead of 'like a teddy bear').

Encourage your toddler to speak by asking simple questions such as 'What is that?' Avoid interrupting her. You can encourage her to use words to express herself, by not responding to requests when she uses gestures alone. But make sure you are not expecting too much.

learning social skills

Full of charm, your toddler is a joy to watch and to be with. Many people, inside and outside the family, are now important in his life. He interacts with them in different ways according to how comfortable he feels with them and his humour at the time. All these encounters influence his social development.

Attachments and relationships

By this age, your toddler's personality shines through strongly, and he is likely to be happy and energetic much of the time. He may have become less cuddly than he used to be, but he is attached to you, and probably to several other people too.

The important attachments that your toddler is forming at this time are vital to his well-being and his development.

He may not always pay attention to you when he is busy playing, but he still senses where you are. He plays more contentedly when you are there.

If you observe his behaviour in the park, you may see him go off happily to explore, returning at intervals to the bench where you are sitting. In effect, he uses you as a secure base from which to launch his independent activities. If you move away from the bench without telling him, he will not like it and may panic.

At one year of age, your toddler may be shy with strangers, but this gradually changes. By 18 months, he is likely to be more outgoing with both adults and children, and he may play happily with other children. However, children vary a great deal. Do not worry if your toddler is still reticent or rarely plays with others.

Awareness of others

From his first birthday onwards, your toddler is more self-aware. If he looks in a mirror, he knows that it is his face he is looking at. He also becomes adept at reading other people's expressions. If he wants to know what you think of a stranger (perhaps the doctor you are taking him to), then he looks to you for your reaction. In the same way, he may put a hand on the doorknob, as he checks your face to see if it is safe to open a door. This is called 'social referencing', and your toddler is in effect tailoring his response to yours. From now on, you may be unable to hide your feelings from him.

Your toddler can do this because he has more social insight. Around now, a part of the brain called the orbito-frontal cortex (see page 63) is developing fast. This is often called the social brain. Almost all of it develops after birth, not in the womb, and matures until the age of 2 or 3. What is interesting is that development of the orbito-frontal cortex relies on a child's relationship with others. In the absence of love and security, this relatively small but vital bit of brain may hardly grow at all.

Bad behaviour

To provide security, the love that you lavished on your baby needs to continue during his toddlerhood. On the whole, it is not difficult to sustain a loving relationship with your child, but toddlers do not always behave socially, and sometimes their behaviour is difficult or even aggressive. When your toddler does wrong, he has to be told that his behaviour is not acceptable because this is how he will learn right from wrong. But make it clear that it is his behaviour that you do not like, not he himself.

Shyness

Many toddlers are sociable, but others are very shy. They fear certain social situations, and forcing them to confront one of these can trigger real fear. The cause of shyness is uncertain, but it may be partly genetic. It can be comforting to remember that sometimes very intelligent toddlers are the most shy and sensitive. One simple explanation is that it is their sensitivity that enabled them to become clever.

There is no alternative to accepting your shy toddler as he is. Even so, there is a lot you can do. Try not to criticize him. Making fun of a child's shyness or forcing him to mix can be cruel and is likely to upset him and make things worse. Telling him that boys are not meant to be shy is also counterproductive.

Give your toddler love and security, so that he can feel safe. In time, he will outgrow his shyness, but to do so he needs your unconditional love and acceptance. Try not to be impatient. This is hard if you are a naturally gregarious person and your child is not. However, in this instance, as in so many other respects, you have to respond to him as he is, not as you might like him to be.

the independent spirit
18–24 months

what is she like?

Your toddler now sees herself as a person separate from you, and from 18 months is likely to be much less biddable; many parents dread the so-called 'terrible twos'. On the plus side, she is developing fast intellectually and emotionally, and her learning really takes off as she approaches her second birthday.

Making the connections

While not much appears to change on the outside, the period between 18 and 24 months is an extremely active stage of intellectual maturation.

By the time your toddler reaches her second birthday, her brain has developed a complex branching network of cells that bears a very close resemblance to an adult's, and the number of synapses, or connections, between cells is at its maximum. Now each nerve cell or neurone has an average of some 10,000 to 15,000 synapses.

From this time onwards, intellectual development depends upon selective pruning of the synapses that are not needed and reinforcement of the ones that are. The stimulation that you give your toddler has a vital bearing on which synapses go and which ones stay.

Primed for advanced learning

Bursting with energy and curiosity, your toddler is primed for learning. She can concentrate well on what interests her. She is also more coordinated than ever before. Towards the age of 2, if not before, she is ready for potty-training.

The speech area of her brain in particular develops rapidly around now. Her new vocabulary extends her thinking. From 18 months or so, your toddler is able to

categorize things and predict events. She has a more sophisticated sense of time and remembers things better. She also makes good use of what she has learned. If she can't pick up a small toy out of a cup, she turns it upside down because she knows that gravity can help.

Thinking and planning

Your toddler's mind emerges strongly now. As well as exercising some logic, she has insight into other people's thinking. She appreciates the difference between animate and inanimate objects and can show kindness.

At the same time, your toddler enters a very creative and imaginative phase. This is thanks to her understanding of symbolism. She may for instance make a shoebox into a bed for a teddy bear, and put many other things to new uses. Now she can make the most of pretend games, and, because she can plan as well as concentrate for much longer, these may occupy her happily for some time.

Emerging independence

Charming and funny as your toddler is most of the time, her journey to independence is not a perfectly smooth path. Towards the age of 2, negativity becomes part of the emotional landscape as she finds her own identity as an individual separate from you. She will want to feed herself, dress herself and do many other things, not all of which she is physically capable of doing yet. When you intervene to give her a hand, she is likely to use her new favourite word, a definite and resounding 'No!' Sometimes, helping your toddler takes extra tact and patience on your part.

ACHIEVEMENTS AT 24 MONTHS

At 24 months, your toddler

- may use a tricycle, but without pedalling properly
- can walk quickly
- can break into a scuttle
- can walk upstairs and downstairs, using two feet per tread
- can climb most things
- can sit and rise from a chair
- can kick a ball without falling over
- can turn the pages of a book one by one
- can build a tower of six or more bricks
- can copy a straight line
- may wash her own hands
- can put on socks and shoes
- may open doors with the handle
- may have strong likes and dislikes when it comes to food
- may wake in the night or very early in the morning
- is very active
- is in a highly creative phase
- has some basic logic
- can concentrate well
- can remember what happened in the recent past
- understands a huge number of words
- makes three-word sentences
- uses pronouns
- makes plurals from singular words
- knows her own gender
- recognizes herself in photos
- can be very uncooperative
- has increasingly frequent tantrums

nourishing your toddler

Your toddler's rapid development means that his brain is now burning as much energy, in the form of glucose, as an adult's, so it will come as no surprise to learn that he needs good nutrition.

Vital food and drink

Your toddler needs a good breakfast to power his day. Apart from main meals, he may need snacks. For the sake of his teeth, keep sugary foods to a minimum between meals. Cheese and crackers are more tooth-friendly than chocolate biscuits or raisins.

Appetites vary, and sometimes busy children have little interest in food. As long as your toddler is active and growing, then all is probably well. The brain needs water too, so let your toddler have water whenever he is thirsty.

There is no need to push fluids when he does want any. Too much to drink can even lower intellectual performance.

Your child requires many different vitamins and minerals. Iron is a vital element, not just to stave off anaemia but also for mood and concentration. About 80 per cent of toddlers have diets lower in iron than they should be, and 15 per cent of those are seriously at risk of iron deficiency. Meat, fish and green vegetables are all good sources of iron. The mineral is absorbed better if vitamin C is taken at the same time, so a glass of orange juice with meals can help.

Essential fatty acids

Omega-3 and omega-6 fats, known as essential long-chain fatty acids, play an important role in many different body processes, and they especially help eye development, behaviour, concentration and learning. Research shows that children with hyperactivity, dyslexia and similar problems can improve when given extra essential fatty acids.

These fats could help all children, though this is still unproven. Two to three servings a week of oily fish such as mackerel, salmon and sardines are probably enough. Omega-3 essential fatty acids are also found in white fish, walnuts, green leafy vegetables and soya, so a varied diet is important. You could also consider an over-the-counter supplement of omega-3 and omega-6 fatty acids.

Persuasion

Getting a toddler to eat what is good for him can be a tall order. Set a good example and adopt a low-key approach. Keep emotional conflict away from mealtimes. Serve a variety of foods to educate your toddler's palate as well as fuel his growth. There is no need to insist he cleans his plate. Helpings are arbitrary and you cannot know how hungry he is. Besides, toddlers can be negative, and he may refuse on principle. If your toddler is hungry, he will eat this meal or, if he does not like it, the next one.

Table manners

As long as you cut up some of his foods, your toddler can use cutlery, though fingers help too. You cannot expect tidy table manners yet, but most children have some sense of occasion, and it is good to eat out sometimes. Keep things simple; a long meal with several courses can be too much.

Toddlers can take their time when they feel like it. Dawdling is infuriating for a parent but just take it in your stride. If you consider that the meal is over, calmly take the plate away and tell your child he can get down.

Obesity and attitudes to food

The soaring rates of childhood obesity are naturally of great concern to parents, but there is never any reason to restrict a growing child's food intake. All you need is the right approach. Do not give food as a reward or withhold it as punishment. Try not to talk about diets and weight loss in front of a child. Instead, foster a healthy attitude to food. It is fuel for the body and often it tastes nice too. That is all.

feeding the senses

Now your toddler is both clever and curious. She can concentrate on what interests her but is easily distracted. Her attention is single-channel, so keep distractions to a minimum. You may notice that when she is engrossed in playing she ignores you totally. She is not necessarily naughty, just too busy to listen.

Teaching tidiness

Do not leave all your toddler's toys out at the same time. Safety considerations apart, there is the risk of her getting bored if everything is all over the floor. It is also good for her to look after her toys and put them away when she has finished. Few toddlers are naturally tidy, so she will not learn this overnight. You can help by turning it into a useful game if, for instance, you put all the blue bricks in the box while she tidies away the red ones.

Groups and categories

Now that your toddler understands categories, you can get her to find or put things away by group, for example all the farm animals. She can also learn which things go together, like shoes and socks, and cups and saucers. Playing picture lotto can be an enjoyable way to learn about matching things and will also help her memory and concentration.

Shapes, textures and colours

Toddlers have a keen interest in comparing things and fitting things together, so she will still enjoy shape-sorters as well as tray jigsaw puzzles. She may also like to thread big beads, or use popper-beads and other toys that fit together.

Different textures and colours are important now. Your toddler will enjoy painting on an easel. Towards her second birthday, she may hold her paintbrush in a more adult grip, but even so her brushstrokes will be random, and she may use fingers as well. Prepare for mess. If you are constantly fretting about the state of the house and her clothes, it may inhibit her creativity. Painting outside can work on a fine day, as can letting your toddler paint just before her bath.

Clay and sand

Your toddler may also enjoy clay now, if it is soft enough for small hands. The different colours are fun, as is the sensation between her fingers. She will soon learn how to flatten a lump of clay into a disc, stretch it out, roll it into a cylinder, and then mash it all together so that she can start again. Whatever the shape your toddler makes out of clay or dough, sooner or later she learns an important scientific principle – that the amount of clay remains the same.

A similar principle applies with sand play, even though sand is completely different from clay. In a sandpit, your toddler can pour sand from one container to another, and just stick her fingers in it. If there is water nearby, she may try to make shapes. Like clay, sand often requires both hands and therefore stimulates both sides of the brain, which benefits development (see also page 117).

Bathtime play

Your toddler may also like playing in the bath. There are many different toys for use with water, but simple beakers, ducks and other floating toys are often favourites. You can also get stick-on shapes that can be applied to tiles or the side of the bath and lift off easily when play is over.

Imaginative play

You can help your toddler by giving her opportunities to develop her senses. You do not need to stimulate her all the time, however. Her own imagination really soars from 18 months onwards, and pretend play will occupy much of her attention for many years to come. A rich make-believe world is important for a growing child. Research even suggests that children who don't have much make-believe play get more stressed as adults, possibly because they have not learned to be imaginative.

Playing house is a lot of fun. There are times when your input is a boon, and others when a teddy and a toy tea-set are all she needs. A play kitchen, play house or tent allow many opportunities for pretend play. If you don't have any of those, you can customize a huge cardboard box or drape an old sheet over a table or over a line in the garden to make a house or a tent. If possible, help your toddler to use natural materials such as branches to make shelters. In this way, she will enjoy touching different materials and will see that not everything has to be pre-fabricated.

Making things

She needs your help to make things, especially if cutting or glueing is involved. If you are making a toy garage out of a shoebox, say, let her decide what it should look like, even if you have to cut out the doors and windows. Talk too about real-life garages you have seen together. This exercises your toddler's powers of observation and her memory.

Construction toys such as Duplo are valuable. Help your toddler to play but don't take over. She may need you to start the ball rolling by showing her how to make houses, trucks, animals or robots out of these versatile bricks, but she will soon get the idea and let her imagination loose.

If you have a son, do not be dismayed if he makes pretend guns out of his construction toys. He may not own a gun, but nearly all children have seen pictures of one, and little boys often make guns out of bricks, sticks or whatever comes to hand. There is no point trying to stop him, even though you may want to point out that real guns are very dangerous and would not be toys.

Books

Toddlers of this age generally enjoy a variety of books, some sturdy enough for them to have themselves and others that need care, which you can look at together. Talk to your toddler about what you read together, and she will soon point to pictures in the book. She may also want to turn the pages. Teach her to be gentle, and soon she will be able to turn pages singly without tearing them.

Music

Contrary to some parents' expectations, early exposure to music is unlikely to turn children into budding geniuses, but all the same it can benefit their development.

Music can certainly be a source of pleasure, especially if you listen and move to music with your toddler. Music helps children's sense of rhythm, which is important for learning language and for their physical development, especially balance and coordination.

Listening intently boosts a child's attention and focus, and may improve memory. The act of sitting still demands considerable muscle control – even more than moving about. This means that you should not expect a young child to sit for longer than she wants to, since she will get fidgety and fed up, which would defeat the object. Also, do not leave music on all the time. Too much background music can affect a toddler's concentration, especially if it is loud. There should be a choice of whether to listen or not.

There is little doubt that, under the right conditions, music has the power to lower stress and improve mood, possibly by increasing the production of feel-good chemicals in the brain. You will probably find that your toddler sings along sometimes. This too may be good for her. Research shows that singing can raise levels of antibodies, so it may even boost the immune system.

Toddlers of this age are too young to learn to play a musical instrument properly, but they can still have fun with toys that make noise.

potty-training

In reality, training a toddler to use the potty has nothing to do with his intellect, though passing the potty-training milestone is a mark of the maturity of his nervous system. And, of course, it is important to parents. However much you may want your child to be out of nappies, you cannot rush the process.

Timing it right

You have to choose the right moment for potty-training, because your toddler can only perform satisfactorily once his nerves have developed enough myelin and he is able to feel that his bowel or bladder is full. Since development proceeds from the top down (see page 23), this is often later than parents imagine.

Even in young babies, the bowel and bladder empty rhythmically rather than in a constant stream. Thanks to a gut reflex, a feed tends to make the bowels move. If you are good at timing, you can catch your baby's stools in a potty from an early age. But this teaches your baby little. The baby is not becoming potty-trained this way – you are.

In general, children become clean before they are dry. By 18 months, many toddlers are aware of passing urine or faeces. By the age of 2, some are clean and dry in the daytime, but many don't become potty-trained until 2½ or even later. This tendency can run in families. Girls are frequently out of nappies sooner than boys, but children vary a great deal. Night-time control comes later, so your toddler may need a nappy when he goes to bed at night until he is about 3.

Beginning to potty-train

The important thing is not to compel your toddler. At this age, he is likely to be contrary, so any attempt at force will backfire. Wait for him to show that he is aware of his bowel movements. He may, for instance, squat down, wrinkle his nose, flap his hands urgently or make some other gesture to indicate that a motion is on its way.

Explain to him what a potty is for and put one within reach. If you have stairs, consider having a potty on each level of your home. Any potty will do. There are few advantages to novelty potties, like those that play a tune. For a boy, choose one with a high front to minimize spraying, as his penis is likely to rise when he urinates.

If the environment is warm, leave his bottom half bare to make it easier to sit on the potty in a hurry. The summer near or after your toddler's second birthday is often a good time to begin potty-training, especially if you can use the garden. Seeing his own stream of urine (or his stool) actually helps your toddler to make the link between his body sensations and the final product.

If your toddler is reluctant to sit on the potty, put him back in nappies and try again a week or two later.

Using the potty

Many parents encourage their toddler to sit on the potty for a short while after meals, when a bowel action is most likely. Remember, however, that any pressure on your part is likely to undermine your efforts. Your toddler may lose interest and wander off. If he is reluctant to sit on the potty, put him back in nappies and try again a week or two later.

When your toddler eventually produces a motion in the potty, praise is in order, but don't overdo it. Using a potty does not make him 'good', and equally the many lapses that will no doubt occur before he is toilet-trained do not mean that he is 'bad'.

Old towels are useful for mopping up mishaps, and your toddler can sit on one when not wearing his nappy. It is a good idea to take pull-up nappies or trainer pants with you when you go on outings.

Using the toilet

Toilets are more intimidating than potties and are often very high. Your toddler may therefore favour the potty until he is 2½ or even 3. When he seems ready for the toilet, make it easier for him by providing a toddler seat and a step.

At 2 years of age, boys usually urinate sitting down, but sooner or later your son will want to stand up, even if there is no male in the household to imitate. Standing is much less messy in a toilet, so there is no need to encourage him to stand at the potty. In fact, boys are often ready to use the toilet, at least for urinating, sooner than girls.

mastering movement

Your toddler may stumble if the ground is uneven, but on the whole she is now much steadier on her legs. Her coordination has improved so much that she can do a number of things while on the move.

Controlling large movements

Until she reaches the age of 2, your toddler can still be clumsy at times, but for the most part she is becoming better coordinated, and she can be careful when the situation demands it. You can help her to gain better control over large muscle movements by encouraging her to use playground equipment in the park. Bigger toys, such as tricycles and sit-on trucks, are also good, although she does not yet have the coordination needed to pedal properly. Playing with a large ball or using a trampoline will enhance her movement too.

When you go out, let your toddler walk some of the time instead of sitting motionless in her pushchair, where she cannot exercise her legs and arms, still less satisfy her curiosity about the things around her. You may still want to take the pushchair with you, in case it becomes too much for your toddler and she does not want to walk back.

Acquiring coordination

Many activities, such as constructing various objects, refine your toddler's hand–eye skills (see pages 98–100). You can also help her coordination by involving her in simple tasks around the house. She wants to be big, so she may enjoy helping to the lay the table, as long as you do not get upset by the occasional mishap.

At this age, many toddlers exhibit a slight trembling of the hands, for instance when playing. Stress or excitement can make the trembling worse. If your

Bigger toys such as tricycles and sit-on trucks can help muscle control, although your toddler does not yet have the coordination needed to pedal properly.

toddler's movements are normal in other ways, then there is unlikely to be a problem; any trembling should no longer be evident by her second birthday or soon afterwards.

Moving both sides

By now, your toddler almost certainly favours one hand over the other. Even so, using both sides of the body can assist development, not just with muscle control, but also with general brain power and understanding. This is because both sides of the brain are important, so it is good to stimulate them both (see also page 117).

Get your toddler to copy you as you touch and name different parts of your body, such as the eyes, ears, nose, chest, belly button and so on. Stand in front of your toddler and do this with your right hand as she copies you with her left, giving her help if she needs it. Repeat the process with your left hand and her right. You can end by doing the sequence a third time with both hands simultaneously.

Splashing about

Water offers resistance to her limbs. Going swimming at a local pool, using a paddling pool in the garden and visiting the seaside are all beneficial. At the beach, your toddler may enjoy running in the sand, which gives a different sensation and exercises different muscles from those that are used when running on firm ground.

Armbands are useful when taking your toddler to the pool or the seaside. Make sure you have the right size for her, since they can slip off if they are too big; some children positively enjoy taking them off and throwing them about. Swimming jackets with floats are ideal for giving a toddler confidence in the water. They also provide some insulation, so the water will feel less cold to your child. Some jackets have removable floats, which means that you can adapt the amount of buoyancy to suit your child by removing or adding floats as the occasion requires.

Do not rely on rings and novelty inflatables such as animals, since a young child can easily slip out and let go. Tie back long hair so that it doesn't get caught up in something and drag your toddler underwater. Even with all these precautions, there is no substitute for supervising your child constantly, and holding on to her if she is out of her depth. Toddlers are vulnerable to drowning because they can't appreciate the dangers of water. That said, there is a lot of fun to be had in the water, and a toddler's development of movement and coordination can really benefit.

discovering identity

Watch closely and you will see that your child evolves his own tastes and style. Certain things please him, some even fascinate him, yet they may hold no special appeal for other children. This results from the unique combination of his genetics and his environment.

Early preferences

Your toddler's early preferences are interesting, and may or may not reflect yours. Occasionally, it is possible to predict from early on where a child's future interests may lie. But do not attach too much weight to his favourite things now. These may change, and every child needs to develop in his own way without being pigeonholed at an early stage.

Right-handed or left-handed?

Around the time of your toddler's second birthday, he is likely to use one hand more more frequently and more instinctively than the other, though some children do not seem to show a final preference until they are at least 4. Even so, ultrasound scans suggest that handedness is probably fixed well before birth.

The right side of the brain controls the left half of the body and vice versa. Handedness relates in some way to which side of the brain is dominant, but there is no straightforward link between left and right.

Left-handed parents are more likely to have a left-handed child, although in general right-handed offspring are more common, and most left-handers are born to right-handed parents. For reasons that are obscure, twins are more likely to be left-handed than singletons, and boys are more likely to be left-handed than girls.

Let your child be

You can often tell which side your toddler prefers by watching him as he holds a crayon, uses a spoon, kicks a ball, or posts shapes through the corresponding holes in a box. Or you could observe which ear he uses for listening to a music box, and which eye he uses to look through a telescope. Even so, laterality, as it is called, is rarely absolute. There may be a few activities that left-handers prefer to do with the right hand, and vice versa.

It is important to let your child follow his instinct instead of persuading him to use one hand rather than the other. His overall ability and dexterity matter far more than the issue of which hand or foot he uses.

RULES AND BOUNDARIES

As your toddler acquires a growing awareness of his separate identity, learning about rules and boundaries is important. So, too, is developing a sense of right and wrong. These do not come naturally to your toddler, so again you need to explain the reasons behind them. You could talk through how the people affected might feel if, for instance, you took someone else's seat on a train or played with another child's ball in the park.

At this age, your toddler is brutally honest and is unable to lie or hide his feelings. He is also instinctively trusting, so strangers hold no fear for him. For his own safety, teach him not to talk to adults whom he does not already know unless you are with him. In this way, he can learn about 'stranger danger' without having to distrust everyone.

learning language

Now your toddler's main means of communication is speech, which demonstrates how far she has progressed since babyhood. All the same, children vary a great deal. By the age of 18 months your toddler could have up to 150 words in her vocabulary, or there may be as few as six.

Understanding others

Your toddler is able to understand much of what you say, and knows the words for parts of the body and common household objects. Even if she does not know the name of something, she often appreciates what it is used for.

You can extend her knowledge by introducing her to new words. You can stretch her understanding gently with simple requests that contain two information words, such as 'Put the cup on the table, please.'

By now, toddlers have acquired a grasp of time and know the meaning of 'later', 'now' and 'not now'. They may understand prepositions such as 'on'. You can use actions to help your toddler grasp more difficult ones, such as 'over', 'behind' and 'through'.

Making words and sentences

As a rough guide, your toddler can probably speak about 40 words and make simple two- to three-word sentences. Encourage her to ask for the things she wants instead of simply pointing to them.

Your toddler's pronunciation is not perfect, of course, but she can make herself understood. At 2, she may still mispronounce common consonants, such as 'w' and 'r', even though she can easily spot the difference when you speak.

Encouraging language development

Young children who receive too little stimulation have a tendency to speak late and may have a poor understanding of what is said to them. You can encourage your toddler's language development by spending time in conversation with her, making eye contact when you speak. Use tone of voice and gestures to hold your toddler's attention and to reinforce what you are saying.

As time goes by, your toddler will respond more readily and coherently when you speak to her. She will also initiate conversation. Be sure to reply with more than just a grunt or an 'Oh'. She needs encouragement when she speaks, or even when she points to an object. Extend your toddler's word power by amplifying what she says. If she points to the dish on the floor and says 'doggie', you could respond by talking about whether the dog is hungry or thirsty, and mentioning what it likes to eat.

Do not correct your toddler's pronunciation overtly. It is more constructive if your reply contains the word she mispronounced but with that word spoken correctly. If she says 'kak', you can respond with 'Yes, the cat is grey and white, isn't she?' By the time you toddler is this age, it is preferable to avoid using a lot of baby-talk, and don't copy her mispronunciations, however charming they may sound.

Reading and playing games

Read and look at books together. It does not matter if your toddler always wants the same one. As long as there is a choice, she will move on to another one when she is ready.

Play simple games together. Hide-and-seek can extend your child's grasp of concepts. Songs and nursery rhymes are helpful too, since they emphasize the rhythms and sounds of speech. Many toddlers like listening to audio tapes and CDs. Singing to your toddler is better than relying on lots of bought material, because you can use gestures to hold her attention and to convey meaning, but a variety of listening matter is good.

Language problems

Delays in speaking are common and do not always signify a problem. Your toddler is more likely to have a genuine language problem if she:
- is more than a year late in mastering sounds that other children make
- uses mainly vowel sounds
- shows little interest in communicating at 18 months
- does not understand simple requests at 18 months
- does not point to familiar things at 18 months when you ask where they are
- mainly echoes what she hears you say at 2 years

- is hard to understand at 2½ years
- omits or swaps consonants after the age of 3
- sounds monotonous, nasal or too loud

If you think your toddler has a language problem, see your health visitor promptly. Since children learn language by imitation, the most likely cause is a hearing difficulty, and the first step is usually a hearing test. Your toddler may also need to be assessed by a speech and language therapist.

emotional intelligence

At 18 months, your toddler is charming, open, naïve, and interested in things. He has noticed that other people do not always think the same way he does – a vital step in developing emotional intelligence.

Logic and thought

During these 6 months, your toddler acquires some basic logic. But some of the things he thinks of as cause-and-effect are linked only because they happened at the same time. When you see examples of this, you can talk things through, making use of his powers of thought to extend his understanding.

Children frequently mimic things they see adults doing. Your toddler does not always need to know the reason why you do what you do, but it is much better for his intellectual development when, instead of saying nothing, you take time to explain why you need to hang a wet towel on a rail, for example. He may not totally grasp your explanation, but it is worth a try.

Self-awareness, egocentricity and confidence

From 18 months, a child is more aware of himself as an individual. He recognizes himself in the mirror and in photographs. Towards his second birthday, he knows his own gender, though probably not his age. Soon he is proudly announcing to all that he is a boy.

Your toddler is still egocentric, which is normal. While he is aware of the fact that other people have needs, his own are still paramount. When he feels less confident, he may use a teddy, a blanket or some other comfort object. There is no harm in this, and he will stop using it once he outgrows the need. Meanwhile, you would do far more damage by forcing him to give it up.

Negativity

Your toddler's behaviour is not always cooperative. This becomes more obvious towards his second birthday, and it is a normal part of his development as an individual. Sometimes he just wants to do things all by himself. He may not be able to do up his trousers, but despite his tears of frustration he may still resent your help. Thoughtful handling is needed during this phase.

TODDLER TANTRUMS

A tantrum is an uncontrolled outburst of temper. Over a period of several minutes, your toddler may scream, kick, stamp his feet, hold his breath and even throw himself to the ground for good measure. The peak time for tantrums is 18–36 months. While not all toddlers have frequent tantrums, most two-year-olds have at least one a week. That is because they are easily frustrated and have limited understanding of why they can't have something when they want it.

There is nothing you can do during a tantrum other than make sure your child comes to no harm. Reasoning or, worse, smacking would be useless. Your toddler is literally beside himself with rage, so keep calm and wait until it subsides. If possible, minimize the attention you give during a tantrum. Your child may give up if he has no audience. Above all, do not give in to your toddler because of a tantrum. If he was not allowed an ice-cream before, he should not get one now.

the problem-solver
24–36 months

what is he like?

Children of this age vary a lot, because their personalities differ, as do their rates of development. Also, depending on their circumstances, each child has slightly different life experiences. The young child who has never seen snow, for instance, cannot know that it feels cold, still less what fun it is to slide on.

Planning activities

By the time he reaches the age of 2, your child will have acquired a useful understanding of the world. Now that he has a good memory and understands the concept of time, he is able to draw on previous experiences to plan his future activities. He can plan-do-and-review, enabling increasingly complex play.

From around the age of 2½, he may also give a run-down of his activities aloud, even if he frequently plays on his own these days. As ever, language and thought are closely connected. Verbalizing helps him to crystallize his thinking and refine his actions.

Planning ahead also involves long-term dreams, which is why, some time around their third birthday, many children begin to talk about growing up and becoming firemen, police officers, and so on. Sometimes their ambitions are less realistic. There is no need to be concerned if your toddler announces that he intends to marry Mummy when he grows up, since this kind of thinking reflects a common flaw in a young child's logic.

Organizing and solving

These errors apart, a child of this age is rather a good thinker. He likes his world to be organized. When it is not

predictable, he tries to discern a pattern to make sense of events. He frequently thinks things through, using logic supplemented by an active imagination that allows him to see different possibilities.

Thanks to a synthesis of curiosity and experience, a toddler enjoys solving a variety of problems. He will appreciate new challenges that allow his problem-solving skills to develop without taxing him too much.

Towards independent living

You will be gratified to discover that, from around the age of 2, your child is able to do so much more than he could a few months earlier. If he is not yet toilet-trained, he soon will be, because, happily, the maturity of the nerves that control bowels and bladder coincide with a child's desire for greater independence.

Your child's pride in his everyday achievements will be all the greater if you make an effort to give him positive feedback. That includes letting him have the time he needs to cope with challenging buttons and zips, rather than hurrying him along or doing it all for him.

Towards sociability

As he approaches his third birthday, your child becomes more sociable. He will talk fluently with you and probably with many other people too. His conversation is likely to consist of question after question and his favourite word is 'Why?'. As well as explaining things to him, you can reinforce notions of right and wrong – important concepts to guide his behaviour.

By this stage, your toddler has become more caring, and genuinely wants to know how others feel and what they think. Your child may play better with other children, and may start making friends outside the family. Before long, he is ready to spend more time away from home, without your constant presence.

ACHIEVEMENTS AT 3 YEARS

At 3 years, your toddler
- has good balance
- can run
- can stand on one foot
- can jump
- climbs well
- goes upstairs using one foot per tread
- can throw a ball
- can pedal a tricycle
- can dress himself, including shoes and some buttons
- draws spontaneously
- can make many basic shapes
- can copy a circle
- is independent in his toileting, except for wiping
- may be dry at night
- may be using the toilet in preference to the potty
- can concentrate well and play in a sustained way
- is very creative and imaginative
- knows many colours
- has powers of logical thought
- may recognize some letters
- may count up to five
- understands almost everything you say

feeding the senses

A 2-year-old puts all the senses to good use. Keenly observant, your toddler will not miss much. She wants to make discoveries for herself and may not take your word for things, preferring to satisfy her curiosity in a more direct way. This is important for her learning, even if at times it is trying for a parent.

Changing perception

All your child's senses are acute and continue to develop. From around the age of 2, she will be able to see all the things that an adult can see, though of course those things do not necessarily have the same significance for her as they do for you. She cannot, for instance, appreciate danger in the same way that you do.

Senses and discrimination

You can help the development of your child's discrimination by not only pointing out objects for her to see, hear or smell but also explaining their purpose or the reason for them. The traffic cones in the road, for instance, are there to protect workmen from cars, while that strong smell by the harbour comes from the many fishing boats. In this way, your child learns to make new connections.

Organizing and learning

Your toddler enjoys organizing, so she will like sorting items by colour, and this also helps her to learn colour names. Even a banal task such as sorting clothes in a pile of washing can be fun for her.

She also has the ability to match objects according to their purpose and size. You can help your child to learn about related objects, for instance by cutting out pictures from old mail-order catalogues and making sets of things that go together.

When possible, let your toddler become involved with, or at least observe, your daily tasks. She will probably be fascinated when you use a calculator, do some gardening or paint a wall. Talk to her about what you are doing too. All these experiences give her the means by which she will be able to solve problems in the future.

Just playing

Not every experience needs to be overtly educational, so do not be concerned if your toddler simply plays rather than looking at picture books or asking questions all the time. Even completing a favourite jigsaw puzzle over and over again is a valuable exercise, because it hones hand–eye coordination. In fact, this kind of undemanding quiet play is also very soothing and can help a child to sleep more soundly at night.

Actually, almost any form of play teaches your child something about concentration and sticking at things. Sustained play is the basis of a vital skill that is essential to effective learning. When you can, let your child play. Naturally you cannot change important plans for the day just because she has got out all her tubs of modelling dough, but, when it is possible, let her enjoy her activities without rushing her or creating distractions.

Sound and music

Help your child to be aware of and distinguish between different sounds, whether they emanate from clocks, bells or car horns. Encourage her to listen to music, and to move around in time to it as well. This will benefit her powers of concentration and her coordination (see also page 101).

Games such as pass-the-parcel are enjoyable, but you can also indulge in musical activities when the two of you are on your own. Put on some music, arrange a bowl of snacks, and you can have an impromptu 'party' as you dance around the kitchen table.

Right and left brain

Babies and young children have symmetrical brains, but among adults one or other side may dominate. Many of those individuals whose left brain is more developed are successful products of formal schooling methods.

Such people are frequently diligent and single-minded, excelling at logic, mathematics and the use of words.

Individuals whose right brain is dominant tend to be more intuitive and creative by nature. They may not shine academically, but they come into their own when it is imagination rather than precision that is called for. These people are likely to become talented musicians or artists rather than engineers.

Of course, both sides of the brain matter. Sorting toys by colour, for instance, is a left-brain activity, while moving to music involves the right brain more. One simple way of stimulating both sides of the brain is to use both sides of the body at the same time, as happens when using a climbing frame, running or playing with modelling clay.

It is important to raise your child in a balanced way, so that her thinking, and the options she has before her, are as wide-ranging as possible.

nurturing creativity

Both girls and boys are highly imaginative, although they may deploy this talent in slightly different ways. Whatever your child chooses to do, the world of make-believe in its various forms can take up a great deal of time, especially from around the age of 2½.

The importance of creating

Creating all kinds of things is an important part of a toddler's play and learning. The child who is creative and imaginative grows into an adult who is good at coping.

Making and building

Thanks to his improving hand–eye skills and concentration, your toddler can now build more complex things. By 2½, he can make a tower of eight or more bricks. By 3, the tower could be much higher (and it may topple over). He can also build more interesting structures, using bricks to make a bridge or to buttress a building. Soon he may be creating whole roads and towns out of blocks, and spending happy hours engaged in this make-believe.

Visual arts

Provide your toddler with paper, crayons and paints. He will also enjoy modelling dough or clay, and using dried pasta shapes to paint or to glue artistically onto card. Think ahead to minimize mess but don't spend ages setting things up for him or you may be disappointed when he moves on to the next activity sooner than you anticipated. Even with the strides your child has made by the age of 2, he still can't concentrate for anything like as long as an older child.

Although you should let your child play at his own pace, a little structure to the day helps prevent boredom. Try to have an outing every day so that your child can experience new things that fire his creativity. Sessions of quiet play with you, perhaps with finger puppets, add variety.

Role-play and make-believe

Role-play is valuable because it gives a child the chance to experiment with, and create, different situations. Keep a variety of old clothes and oddments in a dressing-up box. What you already have at home can be supplemented by cheap jumble-sale items. You may also want to invest in a couple of props, such as a pirate's eye patch or telescope, or a fireman's helmet, to give his play an air of realism.

Sometimes your toddler will want you to take part, while at other times you will be required to stay in the background.

Self-expression and satisfaction

Self-expression makes a child feel good about himself. What he makes does not have to please you or anybody else. It simply has to satisfy the creator. Even so, positive feedback from you goes a long way and can spur him on to new things. Sometimes it may be hard to be complimentary about what he has made, especially if it does not look like anything recognizable, but comments such as 'What a pretty colour' come in handy. Talking with your child about what he makes, or how he makes it, extends his language skills. For instance, when playing with dough, words like 'stretchy', 'round', 'coiled', 'fat' and 'lumpy' can enter the conversation.

Cooking is creative too, and suitable for both boys and girls. Your child can enjoy stirring batter, cutting shapes to make biscuits or icing fairy cakes with you. Here, part of the satisfaction is eating the end-product (as well as sampling the ingredients along the way).

a head for maths

Learning about numbers and what they mean is often easier for young children when they can feel and see the numbers.

What learning maths means

Children vary, but from around the age of 2½ your toddler may be able to recite numbers in the right order. She can remember a sequence of digits long enough to repeat them after you, and by her third birthday she may be able to count up to five. But knowing what numbers are called is not the same as understanding what they represent, still less what can be done with them.

Learning mathematics is a complex business with many facets. Your child's maths learning relies just as much on understanding concepts and groups of things. By 2 or 2½, she is very aware of groups of things like buildings, vehicles and farm animals. She can also see the link between related objects such as socks and shoes, and tables and chairs.

In addition to counting and sorting, your toddler needs to find out about finding patterns, making connections, recognizing relationships between different things, and working with a variety of different measures as well as with numbers. But the complexity of even simple mathematics brings one enormous advantage: there are many activities that help a child learn maths.

Learning numbers

Numbers can be used as names or labels, for instance on the house where you live. They can also act as measures of something, as for example the number of beakers filled with sand. Help your child to notice numbers used as labels in everyday life. You can also help her to count common objects, if she wants to. In this way, she will eventually see that four seashells, say, are still four in number even when you count them in a different order.

Measuring

Using a shape-sorter, playing with sand, using modelling dough, handling cooking ingredients and filling beakers with water are all useful activities for teaching basic maths.

At first, all your toddler needs to understand is 'more', 'less' and 'the same', or 'longer/shorter' and 'heavier/lighter'. A toy tape measure can be fun too, and helps in comparing lengths when you cannot put two objects directly side by side (for instance, park benches), but your child will probably need to be at least 3 years old before she can properly grasp the use of rulers and tape measures.

Many parents are keen to teach their child to tell the time, but there is no rush. Hours and minutes are too complex at this age.

Useful games and activities

There is no point in constructing a timetable to teach your child maths. At this stage, she should learn from enjoyable activities rather than formal teaching. Building blocks continue to be fun, and vital for learning maths (so too are toy trains and snap-together beads). They can be counted, and they can be made into structures that are long or tall, big or small, and so on. The fact that an object can be taken apart into its components is an early lesson in division.

Playing with play money is useful, as long as it is not too complicated. Coins of different denominations confuse some children, but you could play shop with tiddly-winks, buttons or other counters.

Games involving dice give practice at counting and turn-taking. Many children enjoy dominoes, and there are versions with bright colours that aid number recognition.

drawing and writing

You may think of reading and writing as closely related skills; for your toddler, however, it is drawing and writing that are more closely linked.

Coordination and drawing

From about the age of 2, your child may draw spontaneously. His wrists are flexible now, giving him better control of the crayon, although he still holds it in his fist rather than in his fingers. His efforts are unlikely to classify as representational art, and he may need to tell you what he has drawn. All the same, it is good to encourage his creativity with crayon or pencil, just as in other forms of creative and imaginative play (see also page 121). It does not matter if he is not neat and tidy in his drawing. Give him plenty of paper and a place where he is unlikely to damage a valuable table surface.

Walls can prove irresistible, and many young children draw on them by way of experiment. This makes perfect sense to a child who has ever seen wallpaper or had his creations displayed on a wall. But your toddler must learn that walls are not for drawing on.

Between the ages of 2½ and 3, your toddler probably holds a crayon or pencil like an adult, with a pincer grip. Any slight shaking he may have had when younger should have gone by now. As a result, he can do much more. He may not spend long drawing but he draws with great enthusiasm.

Edges and shapes

Around now, your toddler learns that a line can be an edge or boundary, so he can make enclosed spaces. This is a huge leap forward as it means he can make basic shapes. Before, he could only imitate you drawing a straight line, but by his third birthday he can imitate you drawing a circle. He can also copy a circle that you drew earlier. Encourage him even if his efforts are misshapen. If you ask, he may draw you a house or a person. The people may just be heads positioned atop legs, with very basic faces, but they will please him.

Early writing skills

At some point, your toddler will draw loops, scribbles and spirals. He may call it writing. As his coordination improves and he sees more examples of writing, his scrawls may become neater and more organized. You can encourage his hand–eye skills with shape-sorting, doing jigsaw puzzles, building things, and even picking up and collecting small objects, such as shells on the beach or acorns in the park.

In due course, he must learn that writing is more than drawing. In writing, the number of shapes (letters) is limited, and the same ones appear over and over again. Writing means making upstrokes, downstrokes or sideways strokes. Even so, writing only goes in one direction. Letters can be joined up, but they do not have to be. To illustrate these principles, you can point out examples of your own writing on lists, envelopes and cheques. Learning numbers can be part of this, but it is not the same as understanding what the numbers mean (see page 121).

First real letters

A few children begin to write before the age of 3, but do not expect your child to do so. It is normal to simply cover the page with a repetitive pattern. If your toddler wants to know more about writing, you can show him how to make common letters, like 'a', 'b' and 'c'. They should be lower case, as these will be the ones he learns at nursery and school. With a very soft pencil, he may want to copy you, but let him go at his pace.

At this point, it is worth finding out from the nursery or school he is likely to attend which methods they use for forming individual letters, since it will be counter-productive if he later has to unlearn what you teach him.

language and thought

As your toddler's word power improves, so her horizons expand; she can plan as well as comment on her activities – an important part of learning.

Running commentaries

At around 2½, many children give a running commentary on what they are doing. This not only sounds charming but also has the important function of helping your child to carry out a complex sequence of actions.

Understanding others and expressing herself

Your toddler's comprehension is more mature than her speech, and before she is 3 she is likely to understand almost everything you say. But she also has an extensive vocabulary that keeps increasing daily, and she uses her words with fluency and expression.

Your toddler now uses important link words such as 'and', enabling her to make long and complex sentences. She understands the words 'today', 'tomorrow' and even 'yesterday'. Towards her third birthday, she speaks in five-word sentences as a matter of course.

It is no wonder that she now uses speech in preference to other ways of getting her meaning across, such as crying or stamping her feet. She can make herself understood by most people, although naturally her pronunciation is still imperfect. She has trouble, for instance, with consonants at the end of words, or when consonants occur together, and she may lisp too.

Finding out more

Your toddler will probably be very chatty and curious about everything. 'Why' remains one of her favourite words. Most of her questions make perfect sense, such as 'Why is that tree yellow?' (However, some questions are more inscrutable, such as 'Why is door?'). Try not to fob her off when she asks you something. If you say you will answer later, keep your promise. You may know the answer to many of her questions, but when you do not it does no harm to say so. You can then find out.

It does not matter if she cannot use the internet or read the science books on your shelf. The fact that you can do these things teaches her that answers can be found if one knows where to look.

Enriching language and thought

The best thing you can do is talk to your toddler, and that means making time for her. Continue to discuss your daily life. Stretch her language and memory by talking about what she did yesterday or two days ago, for instance. She may not always remember but it will spur her development.

Talk, too, about more abstract topics, such as feelings and moods. This is important for all children of this age, but it may benefit boys most, since they are more likely

The best thing you can do is talk to your child. Continue to discuss your daily life together. Stretch her language and memory by talking about what she did two days ago.

to think in a concrete way. Remember that you can ask questions as well, and these will stimulate your child's thinking and her problem-solving skills. Try a few 'what if?' questions and encourage her to imagine what life might be like if, for example, everyone had a helicopter instead of a car.

Pay attention to what you say in front of your child. Toddlers tend to repeat everything they hear, especially unfamiliar phrases. This is the way in which they enlarge their vocabulary. However, depending on what your child hears, this can include bad language as well as things that you might prefer not to hear repeated in company.

Improving pronunciation and grammar

As in earlier years, don't correct your child's words overtly. It is better to incorporate the right version in your response, as if it were a normal part of the conversation. If she says 'childs sleeped', your reply should use the words 'children slept'.

Some of your child's mispronunciations may be endearing, but on the whole it is advisable not to repeat them yourself, since this could perpetuate the errors. Having said that, in many families it is common for the whole household to adopt the youngest child's version of a common word (such as 'fluvly' for 'flower'), and for this to stick for many years. Provided you only do this for one or two words, it is unlikely to do real harm.

ready for reading

In the same way that mathematics is about much more than just reciting numbers, reading involves more than simply knowing the ABC. Learning to read grows naturally from interacting with others, and from discovering that symbols like pictures and words can hold and communicate meaning.

Teaching reading

Learning to read, in the broadest sense of the term, has its roots in early babyhood. Like learning to walk, it is a continuous process rather than a sudden leap.

Becoming literate should be an enjoyable and interactive exercise, and it should progress at a pace appropriate for each individual child. Ambitious parents are frequently keen for their children to learn to read at an early age, but young children do not generally thrive on formal teaching. You may discourage your child if you press him, since he may form negative associations with books. In addition, if his early attempts do not succeed, he may come to link books with a sense of failure.

Recognizing and remembering

One of the most constructive things you can do to help is to continue reading aloud to your toddler. This reinforces the idea that sounds and printed words can match. Using gestures and exaggerated tones to convey parts of the story, or different voices for different characters, can bring a book to life for your child.

Rhyming books and nursery rhymes are valuable. Their predictability may bore you, but it is an asset because it helps your toddler to memorize the words and meanings.

Let him turn the pages. He may also want to interact with the content, making up parts of the story. When allowed to hold a book on their own, many toddlers babble fluently in mimicry of reading.

Understanding

Have conversations about what you have read, and ask each other questions about the book. This shows that your child has understood, and can link what happened in the book to his own everyday experiences. He may decide to make up a different ending to a story. Being creative means he is interacting with the book.

Developing literacy skills

Many toddlers like to have the same book read to them again and again. This stimulates the development of literacy skills. When you pick up that favourite book yet again, you can pause for a moment on the cover or the title page, and perhaps ask your child what it is about. In anticipation of the delights to come, he may give you the gist of the story in his own words, or simply reaffirm that he really likes this book. During the story, you will find that pausing and asking what happens next brings out a hugely fluent explanation from your toddler. He is remembering rather than reading, of course, but it is still a valuable link in the chain of development.

Have fun with books. When reading a familiar story or rhyme, try leaving out one of the words. You will not have to wait long for your child to protest or to correct you.

Letters and words

Playing with alphabet jigsaws, bricks and magnetic letters all help your toddler to recognize letters. It is also worth pointing out words that can be seen in everyday life, for example in shop signs, food labels and street names. Your toddler will also want to know how his name is spelled. You can write his name on his works of art and on some of his belongings, for instance inside wellington boots.

If your child shows an interest in individual words on a page, use a finger to underline as you read a story to him. When he seems ready, you can also write labels on common objects around the home, such as a bed, a lamp and a table. Use lower-case letters because these should be the ones he learns first.

Enjoying books

Let your toddler know that books are special. It is good for him to have a place just for his books, rather than in the general muddle of the toy-box. Set a good example by reading books, papers and magazines. Households where the adults enjoy books tend to produce children who also have an enduring love of books.

television and computers

Television has brought a whole world of information and entertainment into the home, and has influenced children's lives in a way that few could have predicted just a couple of decades ago. Its impact on a child can go way beyond those hours during which the television set is switched on.

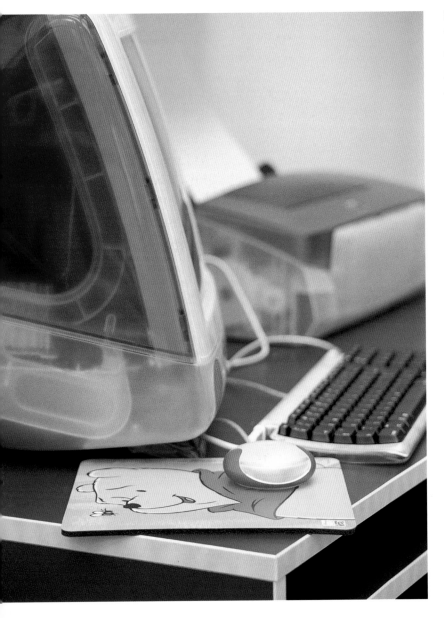

Some benefits of television

Your toddler may become enchanted by particular television programmes. Well-made programmes are a joy to watch and they can contribute to a young child's development.

Judicious viewing has some educational value. However, children learn most from interactive methods, and even age-appropriate programmes can hardly be called interactive. Programmes may not be at the right pace for your child either, which can cause confusion.

Psychological and emotional effects

Long-term exposure to television has been linked with lasting negative effects on children, although there is continuing debate about the exact nature of these effects.

Researchers in the USA found that prolonged television viewing between the ages of 1 and 3 was linked to a higher risk of attention deficit disorder. Other studies have not confirmed this. However, there is evidence that children aged between 6 and 10 years of age who watch violent scenes may grow into angry violent adults.

There is also evidence that frightening programmes are linked with nightmares, and that distressing news programmes and documentaries can cause lasting stress in viewers of all ages. It therefore makes sense to vet very carefully what your child watches.

Computer use can be habit-forming, so many children spend far longer at the screen than parents would like. It can be hard to wrench them away to do other things.

Inactivity and obesity

Television is a compelling medium but a passive one intellectually and physically. Extensive viewing can affect detrimentally a child's posture and activity levels.

Extensive television viewing is also linked with obesity, partly because snacking and viewing go together in many homes. In fact, watching television is so passive that it consumes fewer calories than sitting doing nothing at all, which may be another factor.

Spending a great deal of time in front of the television reduces the amount of time that your child spends out and about, taking exercise, developing social skills and learning language, mathematics and everything else.

What and when to watch

Around 30 minutes a day of watching television, videos or DVDs is probably enough for a child of 2 or 3. If your child watches for a very long period, you may find that she becomes unbearably restless later.

It is a good idea to select in advance of viewing one or two programmes that your toddler likes to watch and that you are happy for her to watch. Obviously, if your child has a television in her own room, you will not be able to exert this kind of control.

Watch with your child whenever possible and talk about the programme afterwards. It is not always easy to stick to selected programmes if your toddler sees that another one is starting at the end of her agreed viewing time, but if you are with her you can distract her with some other activity when it is time to switch off.

Computer games

Some computer games are aimed at very young children, and they are persuasively marketed too, but this does not necessarily make them a good thing for your toddler.

Although we live in a technological era, children do not need to acquire computer skills at such a young age. In due course, all children benefit from knowing what computers can do, but there is plenty of time later for learning about information technology and using a keyboard. Sitting at a terminal tends to encourage poor posture and, even in youngsters, has been linked with repetitive strain injury. Prolonged computer use may affect a child's eyesight too.

Since computer use can be habit-forming, many children spend far longer at the screen than parents would like. It becomes hard to wrench them away to do other things such as playing, socializing and generally interacting with the real world. A few youngsters even refuse to stop for meals and bathing, and become virtual recluses.

Educational value

People who are in favour of computers for the very young maintain that computer games can be educational. They can indeed help a child to develop visual discrimination, muscle coordination and speedy reaction times. Games are more interactive than television and videos. But, rather than exercising your child's imagination, they make use of the games programmer's skills. If you can guide your toddler to make selective use of computer games, they will probably do no harm, and may even do some good, but overall there are better ways of enhancing your child's development.

mastering movement

Your toddler now controls his body in a more sophisticated way, adapting his movements and efforts to the task in hand. While some actions are almost automatic, others demand initiative. His thinking allows him to tackle more complex tasks, and considerable planning can go into a new venture.

Fit for the future

Perfecting and enjoying physical activity now takes up much of your toddler's time. Daily exercise contributes to a young child's all-round development and makes a good night's sleep more likely. No less important is the fact that your toddler is building healthy habits for the future. His lifestyle now could have long-term effects on his heart, bones and brain, for instance.

Achieving a good balance

Movement is natural, and a child's innate curiosity is an important spur to doing things. For the most part, a toddler keeps active without any prompting from you. If anything, you are the one whose energy flags at the end of the day. However, not every young child is physically active. If there are many sedentary distractions, for example, then your toddler may not be as active as she should be. It is up to you as a parent to maintain a balance between physical and less physical pursuits.

Setting a good example is a major part of this, so try to have fun together doing things, whether it is going to the park, having a picnic or raking up fallen leaves.

Motor development

Your toddler's power and coordination are now very good. By 2½ years of age, he walks well, swinging his arms like an adult. He rarely falls, no matter how busy he is. Towards his third birthday, he runs well, can turn while on the go, and knows how to jump, even though he usually uses both feet. Your toddler experiments with new movements, and refines old moves, putting them together in new ways.

Roads and other dangers

His curiosity is intense and at times he may disappear for quite a while in the park or playground, so you need to keep an eye on him. He has little understanding of danger. However, now that his memory is more developed, you can start teaching him the basics of road safety. He will not be ready to cross roads for a long while yet, except when holding your hand, but he is clever enough to take in some explanations about traffic, lights and crossings by way of background to learning proper road drill a bit later on.

Thanks to his powers of observation, he is also ready to understand such things as slippery leaves on pavements, rickety slides and so on, though theory is not the same as practice, and he may not resist the lure of danger.

Your toddler experiments with new movements, and refines old moves, putting them together in new ways.

Ball skills

By the age of 2, your toddler can probably kick a ball without losing his balance, but his aim may be wildly inaccurate for some time to come. When throwing and catching, he holds his arms stiffly, but he takes pleasure in ball games and the practice eventually pays off. As when he was younger, even unsuccessful movements teach him something, as long as he does not become despondent.

Children vary a lot, but on the whole boys are better at ball skills than girls. This is partly inborn and partly environmental. All the same, it is a good idea to play ball with your daughter. Even if neither of you has much aptitude, enthusiasm is catching, and encouragement is good for your child.

Swimming and water movements

Young children love water. Its buoyancy makes movements feel different, and your child exercises slightly different muscles than when on dry land. Some swimming classes take young toddlers as long as a parent comes too.

It is a great way for your child to enjoy himself and gain confidence in the water. However, the experience of a warm swimming pool is very different from a sudden plunge into an icy canal. You cannot therefore rely on lessons taken now to enable him to survive an accidental fall into water.

The language of movement

Almost all your toddler's skills are interrelated. His newly developed control of movement expands his understanding of the world, and his vocabulary as well. Talking to your toddler about his activities before, during and after them helps his word power and his planning.

learning social skills

The brain's orbito-frontal cortex matures well in the third year of life. This is a formative time, in which your toddler acquires new skills and insights that shape social behaviour. When her own instincts and experience don't tell her how to respond, she takes her cue from you or other adults whom she trusts.

Your toddler and other people

By her third year your toddler will have acquired a good sense of herself in relation to the people around her. She may enjoy talking about other family members such as aunts and uncles, and how they relate to her and to others. Encouraging this interest in family and belonging will help her to feel more secure.

At the start of her third year, your toddler is very self-centred, but this begins to change as she approaches her third birthday. She becomes interested in what others are thinking and feeling, especially if they are close to her. Sometimes she checks your facial expression to gauge what is appropriate behaviour.

Strangers are interesting too. Your child may speculate about what they are doing, thinking or feeling. If you see people queuing up for a bus, you can talk about what they are thinking, and how they might feel if the bus turns out to be too full for them to get on.

Your toddler is no longer shy, and may strike up conversations with strangers. For her own safety, it is wise to teach her not to talk to people she does not know unless you are there too.

Growing awareness

By the age of 3, most toddlers are capable of appreciating someone else's point of view and responding to their distress. Girls tend to do this more readily than boys. Praising your toddler for thoughtful behaviour will encourage her to do it again next time.

Naturally, toddlers are interested in other children, and this includes babies. They instinctively know that babies enjoy soft, high-pitched voices and simple repetitive words. Around now, your toddler is ready to mix and play with other children for longer periods of time and to make real friends with children outside the family.

Kindness and sharing

Kindness makes it possible for people to rub along better. It is the stuff that helps to bind societies together, for the good of everyone. Adults know this, but for young children kindness is not a totally natural trait, and at first sight there seems to be little reward for being kind. That perhaps is why toddlers vary so much.

Nevertheless, towards the age of 3, most toddlers are capable of showing consideration for others. Your child may, for instance, be happy to share her toys with another child without being asked. It would be too much to expect her to share everything, however, so before another child visits it can be a good idea to put away her very favourite things and anything else she does not want to share.

Your toddler is now mature enough to take turns. This makes lots of different games possible. Do not expect too much of her, but do make the most of occasions when she is in the right frame of mind for turn-taking.

As she approaches her third birthday, your toddler will probably have developed the maturity and gentleness to help to care for an animal. If you have a pet, she may already understand that it is more easily hurt than she is. Let her take some responsibility, but not too much, for changing the water bowl, say, or giving the cat a saucer of food. But do supervise your pet. Toddlers can be clumsy and impulsive, and can hurt an animal even if there was no intention of doing so.

Rudeness and bad behaviour

Toddlers can cause offence without meaning to. Explain that it is rude to point at people or to get up from a table without asking. Make it clear that it is her behaviour that could be better, and not she who is bad. Do not criticize harshly, and do praise her when she does something right.

Make her feel big by involving her in things like doing simple chores or choosing a present for a grandparent. This makes her feel valued and increases her self-esteem, spurring her on to greater things.

Love and cuddles

In addition to talking about others' feelings, make sure that your toddler is aware what your feelings are. Don't be afraid to show her that you care, by frequent cuddles, and by telling her that you love her. Parents rarely say this too often. Remember that, to your toddler, your love is far more important than anything else you could give.

sex and gender

A toddler is aware of gender and around now may proclaim to everyone that he or she is a boy or girl. Even 10-month-old babies know something about gender. Research shows that they spend more time looking at pictures of babies of the same sex as themselves than of babies of the opposite sex.

Gender differences: general trends

The differences are more than just the obvious anatomical ones. By their first birthday, boys already like noisy games and adventurous play more than girls do. By 3, boys cry less and show fewer intimate gestures than girls. They explore more and are more boisterous. They have better spatial awareness, which is reflected in more advanced ball skills.

Girls talk earlier and often walk and become potty-trained sooner too. They are quieter and more graceful than boys, as well as more patient and cooperative.

The reasons

There are structural differences between male and female brains that may be due to the action of the male hormone

testosterone, which affects the growing brain as well as other organs. But there are other reasons too. Parents treat baby girls and boys differently. Mothers talk more to girls and hug them more. Even when very young, boys tend to be praised for bravery, while girls get plaudits for being pretty or helpful. As parents, we respond to our baby's gender traits, but we create some of them too, an example of the interaction between genes and the environment.

Awareness of genitals and masturbation

Around the age of 2½, children become interested in their genitals. This seems to follow on from potty-training, which depends on an awareness of sensations from the genital area. Because a penis protrudes, male genitals attract more attention, but girls and their playmates are also fascinated by their private parts. Children sometimes show each other their genitals in an entirely natural and innocent way. This is nothing to worry about.

Children of both sexes touch their genitals by way of discovery, and some play with them more than others. If your child masturbates at home, do nothing. If in public, distract your child with something more interesting. This usually works because children often masturbate more when they are bored. There is no need at all for any punishment or to tell your child that this is something dirty or disgusting. Scolding will only make your child feel worse.

AVOIDING GENDER STEREOTYPING

However hard parents try, it is impossible to avoid all gender stereotyping, because there are many influences on a child, including other relatives, books and television. All the same, you can gently guide your child's experiences to avoid many of the negative effects of stereotyping.

If you have a son Cuddle him and encourage him to express emotions. There is no reason why boys can't cry when they hurt. Have one-to-one talks that include abstract and emotional topics. When reading together, ask him what he thinks a character is thinking or feeling, for instance. Help him to play in a sustained way, so that his concentration develops. Play games that involve taking turns. He can still enjoy active games, of course, but also spend time in quiet pursuits.

If you have a daughter Nurture her strengths and praise her for what she is good at. Encourage her to play physical games. She may not have the same zest for football, say, that a boy might have, but she can still enjoy herself. Choose clothing that lets her move freely. Give her chances to play with shapes, puzzles and construction toys. Girls often lack the opportunity, especially as toddlers. Read to her books that show girls and women succeeding. She may not want to become a pilot or a president when she grows up, but it is important to instil a can-do attitude.

starting playgroup or nursery

Pre-school education at a nursery or a playgroup gives your child a fresh environment in which to practise the skills he has learned. There he will also mature in many ways, intellectually, emotionally and socially.

Knowing when your child is ready

Not every toddler is ready for nursery or playgroup at the same age. A child sent too early may be overwhelmed by the experience and unable to make good use of it. As a guide, your child is ready when he can communicate well and is self-reliant enough to be away from you for short periods. If he is still clingy and dependent, leave it a bit longer. You may also want to postpone pre-school if there is a new baby in the family, since your toddler may prefer to stay close to you. If you are not sure, you could ask if he can attend for a couple of trial sessions to see how he copes, before deciding whether to send him every day.

It is a help if your toddler can go independently to the toilet. Many nurseries turn down children who are still in nappies. For this reason, as well as their greater emotional maturity, girls are often ready for nursery before boys.

Choosing a nursery or playgroup

Nursery tends to be more structured and may be attached to a primary school. Playgroups are less formal, but they vary a lot and it is worth looking carefully at what is available in your area. Visit several places, and begin your search in good time, as popular pre-schools fill their places quickly.

Use your instincts. The atmosphere, the physical space, the equipment and whether the children seem happy are all revealing. Ideally, the youngsters will appear to be happily occupied, rather than looking bored or running riot.

When visiting a pre-school, you need to find out the basics like hours and fees, and ask searching questions:
♦ What is the child to adult ratio, and what level of supervision is there?

♦ How structured are the activities? Can children choose what they do when?
♦ Is there a progression in the activities according to the age of the child? Are boys and girls treated the same?
♦ How do the staff deal with bad behaviour?
♦ Are parents expected to help? If so, is there a rota system?

Preparing your child for pre-school education

Take your toddler to see the pre-school. Tell him when he will be starting, but do not give so much detail about pre-school that it daunts or confuses him. Make sure that before the start date he can take off and put on his shoes, and can use the toilet with only a little help. If your toddler has a favourite toy or other cuddly, reassure him that this can go with him to playgroup or nursery too if he wants.

Starting pre-school

The very first morning, even though it may be only a couple of hours long, is nevertheless a significant moment in your toddler's life. As well as any comfort object, take along a bag containing a complete change of clothes, just in case. Mishaps are common, especially at the start.

It may be possible for your toddler to attend part-time for a week or two, just to get used to his new regime. For the first few sessions, you may want to stay with him, but try to melt into the background rather than stay at his side the whole time. When you do leave the premises, always say goodbye and tell your toddler that you will be back later. Although there are often a few tears at first, these soon pass, and before long your child will be making the most of this exciting new phase of his development.

picture credits

Key: ph=photographer, a=above, b=below, r=right, l=left, c=centre.
All photographs by Daniel Pangbourne unless otherwise stated.

Pages 5 & 6l ph Winfried Heinze; 11 ph Dan Duchars; 25 ph Debi Treloar; 26 ph Winfried Heinze; 27a ph Debi Treloar; 27b ph Ian Wallace; 28 © Stockbyte; 32r ph Polly Wreford; 34 ph Winfried Heinze; 35 © Stockbyte; 36 ph Dan Duchars; 39 ph Winfried Heinze; 41© Stockbyte; 42–43 ph Polly Wreford; 44–47 ph Dan Duchars; 49 ph Polly Wreford; 50 © Stockbyte; 52r ph Winfried Heinze; 55 both ph Winfried Heinze; 58 & 59a © Stockbyte; 59b ph Dan Duchars; 65a ph Winfried Heinze; 65b ph Debi Treloar; 78 ph Claire Richardson; 88 ph Debi Treloar/Julia & David O'Driscoll's house in London; 89a ph Debi Treloar; 90–91 © Stockbyte; 96l ph Winfried Heinze; 101r ph Winfried Heinze/Apple Lydon's bedroom – Kate Lydon Interiors, kalershankey@aol.com; 103 ph Winfried Heinze/a family home in New York designed by Susan Johnson of Blue Bench, www.bluebenchnyc.com; 110a ph Winfried Heinze; 110b ph Winfried Heinze/Sophie Eadie's home in London – The New England Shutter Company, www.tnesc.co.uk; 118 ph Polly Wreford; 122 ph Debi Treloar; 123 ph Winfried Heinze/a family home in Brighton – SILENCE creative research design company, www.silence. co.uk; 126 ph Winfried Heinze/Sophie Eadie's home in London – The New England Shutter Company, www.tnesc.co.uk; 127–28 ph Debi Treloar; 131 ph Winfried Heinze/Apple Lydon's bedroom – Kate Lydon Interiors, kalershankey@aol.com; 132, 136–37 ph Polly Wreford.

suppliers

Many of the toys and clothes featured in the photographs are available from the following suppliers. You can buy online or visit their websites to find a store near you.

Cath Kidston
51 Marylebone High Street
London W1U 5HW
020 7935 6555
www.cathkidston.co.uk

Daisy & Tom
181 Kings Road
London SW3 5EB
www.daisyandtom.com

Early Learning Centre
08705 352352
www.elc.co.uk

Holz Toys
The Creamery
Lostwithiel
Cornwall PL22 0HG
0845 130 8697
www.holz-toys.co.uk

John Lewis
08456 049 049
www.johnlewis.co.uk

JoJo Maman Bebe
0870 160 8820
www.jojomamanbebe.co.uk

Mamas and Papas
0870 8307700
www.mamasandpapas.co.uk

Mothercare
08453 304030
www.mothercare.com

resources

Amateur Swimming Association
Harold Fern House
Derby Square
Loughborough
Leicestershire LE11 5AL
01509 618 700
www.britishswimming.org
*Education and certification
programmes for teachers and officials
as well as a Learn to Swim Awards
scheme. Aims to ensure that all have
a chance to learn to swim.*

BLISS (the premature baby charity)
68 South Lambeth Road
London SW8 1RL
020 78209471
helpline 0500 618140
www.bliss.org.uk
*A wide range of information and
support for parents of premature
babies and their families.*

Child Accident Prevention Trust
Fourth Floor, Cloister Court
22–26 Farringdon Lane
London EC1R 3AJ
020 7608 3828
www.capt.org.uk
*A charity committed to reducing the
number of children injured in accidents.
Provides information and advice for
parents and carers on a wide range
of topics, including toys and play.*

**CRY-SIS (help for parents
of crying babies)**
BM Cry-sis
London WC1N 3XX
helpline 08451 228 669
(08451 ACT NOW)
7 days a week, 9am–10pm GMT
www.cry-sis.org.uk
*Provides support for families
with excessively crying, sleepless
and demanding babies.*

Home Dads
0775 254 9085
www.homedad.org.uk
info@homedad.org.uk
*Support group and online forum
for stay-at-home fathers.*

Home Start UK
2 Salisbury Road
Leicester LE1 7QR
0116 233 9955
freephone 0800 068 63 68
www.home-start.org.uk
*A charity with a national network
of trained parent volunteers offering
support to parents who are for a
variety of reasons struggling to cope.*

**International Association
of Infant Massage (IAIM)**
88 Copse Hill
Harlow
Essex CM19 4PP
0781 6289788
www.iaim.org.uk
*Promotes nurturing touch and
communication through training,
education and research, so that
parents, caregivers and children are
loved, valued and respected throughout
the world community.*

La Leche League
PO Box 29
West Bridgford
Nottingham NG2 7NP
helpline 0845 1202918
general enquiries 0845 456 1855
www.laleche.org.uk
*Helps mothers to breastfeed through
mother-to-mother support, education,
information and encouragement, and
promotes a better understanding of
breastfeeding as an important element
in the healthy development of the
baby and the mother.*

National Childbirth Trust (NCT)
Alexandra House
Oldham Terrace
London W3 6NH
0870 4448707
www.nctpregnancyand
babycare.com
*The leading charity dealing with
pregnancy, birth and early parenthood
in the UK, operating at both local
and national levels, and offering
information about and support in
early parenthood choices.*

**National Council for
One-Parent Families**
255 Kentish Town Road
London NW5 2LX
020 7428 5400
www.oneparentfamilies.org.uk
*A charity working to promote the
welfare and independence of lone
parents and their families.*

**National Day Nurseries
Association**
Oak House
Woodvale Road
Brighouse
West Yorkshire HD6 4AB
0870 774 4244
www.ndna.org.uk
*A charity that aims to enhance
the development and education
of children in their early years.
Dedicated to the provision, support
and promotion of high-quality care
and education for the benefit of
children, families and communities.*

National Literacy Trust
Swire House
59 Buckingham Gate
London SW1E 6AJ
020 7828 2435
www.literacytrust.org.uk
*A charity dedicated to building a
literate nation. Although primarily
aimed at professionals, there is
information for parents on gaining
literacy and on the use of music.*

Parentline Plus
020 7284 5500 for general
information on Parentline Plus
and its services.
helpline 0808 800 2222
www.parentlineplus.org.uk
*A charity offering support to
anyone parenting a child. It operates
14 regional offices and provides
telephone and online services.*

Sure Start
Department for Education and
Skills and Department for Work
and Pensions
Level 2, Caxton House
Tothill Street
London SW1H 9NA
public enquiry unit 0870 0002288
www.surestart.gov.uk
info.surestart@dfes.gsi.gov.uk
*A government programme that aims
to deliver the best possible start in life
for every child. It brings together early
education, childcare, health and family
support. Birth to Three Matters is
a framework to support children
in their earliest years.*

**Tamba (the Twins and Multiple
Births Association)**
2 The Willows
Gardner Road
Guildford
Surrey GU1 4PG
0870 770 3305
helpline 0800 138 0509
www.tamba.org.uk
*A charity providing information
and support networks for families
of twins, triplets and more.*

Tumble Tots
Bluebird Park
Bromsgrove Road
Hunnington
Halesowen
West Midlands B62 0TT
0121 585 77003
www.tumbletots.com
*Britain's leading physical play
programme for children, is a
springboard to developing skills for
life through its national network of
Gymbabes and Tumble Tots courses.*

index

acknowledgments

The publishers would like to thank all the clever babies and parents who modelled for us, especially for their patience during photography. Thanks are also due to Daisy & Tom, Holtz Toys, JoJo Maman Bebe and Mothercare for supplying toys and clothes.

The author would like to thank Henrietta Heald at Ryland Peters & Small and Catherine Clarke at Felicity Bryan Literary Agency, both wise beyond their years, and Clare Meadows Atherton of First Steps Nursery, Bramhope, West Yorkshire, for her inspired ideas.